Fae Enchantment

Adult Therapy Colouring Book
by Morgan Fitzsimons

Cover portrait Twilight Enchantment
featuring
Karen Kay ~ Queen of all things Fae
and Enchanter Michael Tingle

2ND EDITION ISBN #978-0-9948768-8-1

Fae Entertainment and Fae Workshop

www.morganfitzsimons.com
www.FaeEntertainment.com
info@Fae-Entertainment.ca

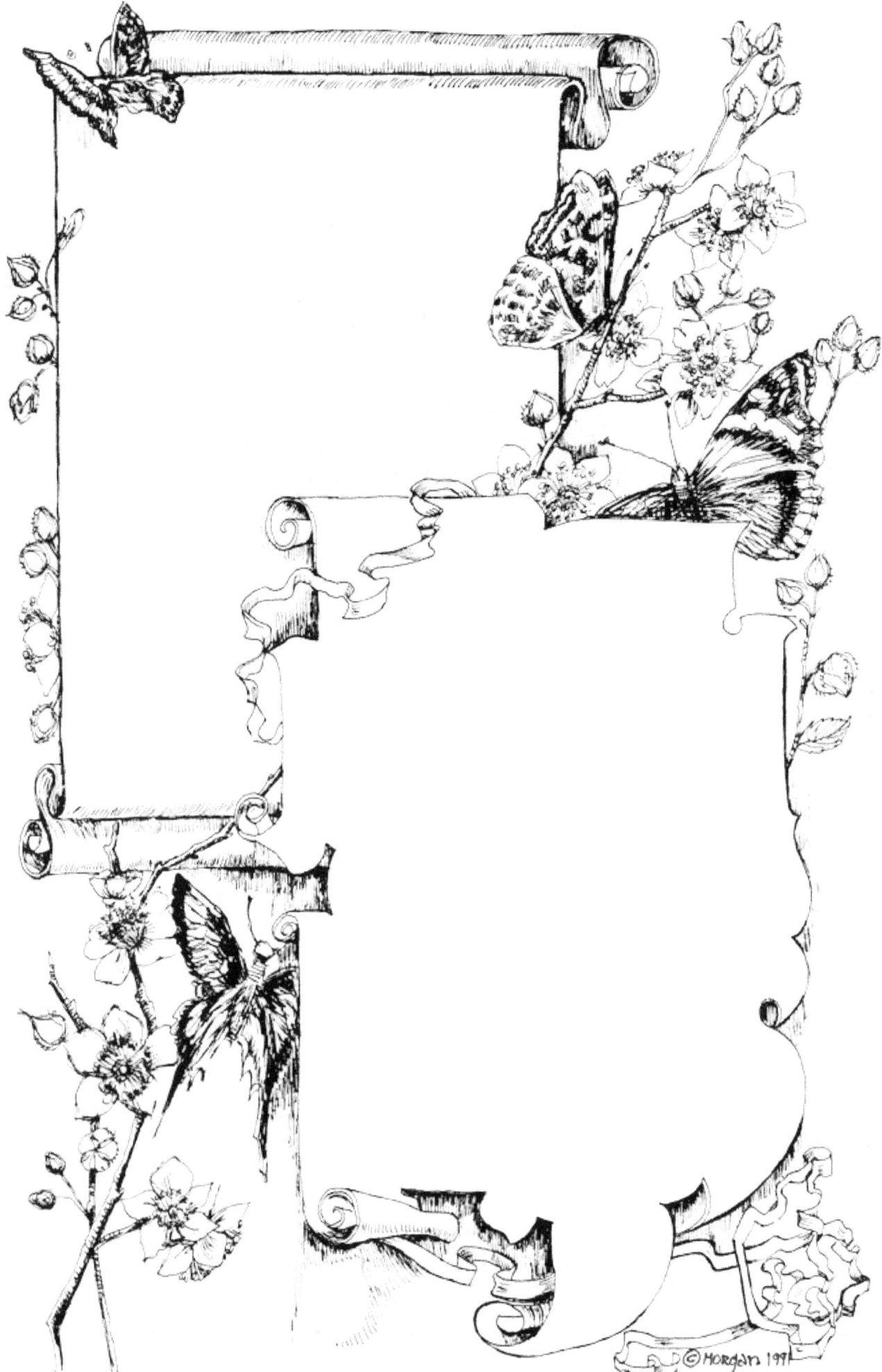

© Morgan 1991

Introduction

People often ask me why I don't appear to exhibit distress, panic or anxiety, and remain calm in the face of most adversity. I am not anything special or super human. I suffer more than my share of pain and difficult circumstances but I find tranquillity and fulfilment in my art. It helps me establish who I am and where I stand in this mixed up world we live in, to be at peace with myself.

Many people have never tried exploring art, believing they lack the skills and ability to create, so I decided to offer an alternative. I put a collection of my images together to tempt people to paint or colour them, in the hope they will go on to explore their own creativity and perhaps find release from the stress of everyday living.

I am unashamedly romantic, and make no apology for the mix prevailing in our ancient heritage, from which come the dreams fuelling my creations, whether paintings, books, designs, poetry or concepts. Dreams pivot on such imagery of what was or might have been, what is and might be, mixed with the longing of the soul for something better and more meaningful, allowing us to touch the heart core of Creation. *'Imagination is more important than knowledge' Albert Einstein*

Had I the Heavens embroidered cloths
Enrought with gold and silver light
The blues the dim and the dark cloths
Of night and light and half light
I would spread the cloths under your feet
But I being poor have only my dreams
I have spread my dreams under your feet
Tread softly for you tread on my dreams
William Butler Yeats

We give dreams expression, reflecting an almost unreal reality, drawn from what went before, mixing with the natural landscape (which should be an extension of the mind), our spirit and soul feeding on the mystery of life.

'I've dreamt all my life, dreams that have stayed with me ever after...they've gone through and through me like wine through water and altered the colour of my mind.' Wuthering Heights Emily Bronte

My dreams are expressed in my books and paintings, reflecting like images in the water, the colour and romance of myths and legend and art and literature from cultures in our ancient past, allowing them to spill over into today.
All things then exist beneath the same sky of stars, viewed from different positions in time and space giving shape and colour to who I am, at one with all that was and is.

'Everything exists everything is true and the earth is only a little dust under our feet.' Celtic Twilight W.B.Yeats

My tranquillity of spirit rests in the constant of today, every morning a new beginning. It is never clearer than in the stillness of dawn's early light, or the twilight when the day ends and night begins, when the world seems briefly silent, the half light shifting, a magical enchanted gateway, a moment of connection, and in the first silence of the early dawn of a fresh new day presenting another chance, a new opportunity to effect change. Ideas flow best in the stillness. My heart is forever young fascinated by the time between and the concept all we have is today, which we are given sufficient grace to embrace.

All things converge in today, the constant time where our heart, soul and spirit exist, though the body is of the earth and unfolding time, eventually returning to dust. It's the only reality, a time between yesterday and tomorrow, and is always new every morning, a new beginning.

Today is all we can live, each moment offering the chance of change. Each new day is another opportunity, for change to grow, to seize the day and be who we are meant to be. I believe we are not only flesh that returns to dust, but beings of an indomitable spirit, an energy connecting with all things spiritual and the beauty and grandeur of all creation in the universe and beyond.

The perception of beauty is personal. There are so many facets, all kinds of beauty, in sounds, visual images, acts and deeds, a changing everlasting weave in the garment of the Creator, the infinite revelation to which the individual soul responds. The heart of beauty is its truth. The more we have truth in us, the more beauty we reflect. Something in all of us loves and responds to beautiful things, though sadly it is a human trait to destroy that which we love, although most of us want to preserve it, many of us destroy it daily. Be true to yourself, live what you believe.

Female beauty can often be misrepresented by depicting narrow stereotypes as desirable perfection, when the truth is, beauty has infinite facets discovered and presented in many ways and sizes, from visual, to feelings of comfort, as different as life itself. My view of beauty may be somewhat old fashioned, but it's an age old concept of identification, with natural values as a yard stick for inspiration.

'I am certain of nothing but the holiness of the hearts affections and the truth of the imagination.' John Keats.

Humanity is compassion. Compassion is the heart's beat. Personal feeling is what makes us what we are. Imagination fuels empathy. The brain imagines, the heart feels. Imagination and compassion are ingrained in our soul. Without these things we are less than human, less than what we can be.

'Imagination is the beginning of creation' George Bernard Shaw

Taking a positive view, beauty is life itself and in all things natural from the North Star and Orion's belt, to earth's hills and woodlands, to the smallest caterpillar. Like many before me my inspiration begins with this.

The beauty of the land on a summer's day is the dream of youth renewed. A walk through the autumn wood of red and gold is evidence of life's miraculous cycles, and the powerful majesty of snow white fields, the misty grey skies of winter heavy with it, and the 'dragon's breath' floating up the valleys of my beloved Wales, the stars emerging in the breathless silence of the half light calling us with their sparkle, are all witness to the beauty of creation.

Even the violent storm or a powerful volcanic rending of the earth, have a compelling beauty. The spring earth bursts into life and colour, awakening from the enchanted dream of winter stirring us to better things. Perhaps we are just a dream, existing in the heart of our Creator.

Beauty is ever-changing in the weave of life, a reflection of majesty and power, the highest revelation we encounter. Something stirs within when we recognise it, accepting the heart's core of truth within it. We can see it in the glittering patterns of light through dancing leaves to the web of the same night stars our ancestors saw. It spreads like the earth making its way into our souls from down the ages and everywhere around us.

The older I get this realm of gold is brighter, and the more beautiful and precious life is, and the heart links forged within unfolding time, present in my constant today, the time between past and future keep my heart soul and spirit forever young, at peace with all things. It is my hope in colouring and painting some of these images, to offer a connection with that same inner tranquillity I found in creating them, and I hope you find the peace that comes with accepting we are part of the beauty in all facets of nature, and at one with the land.

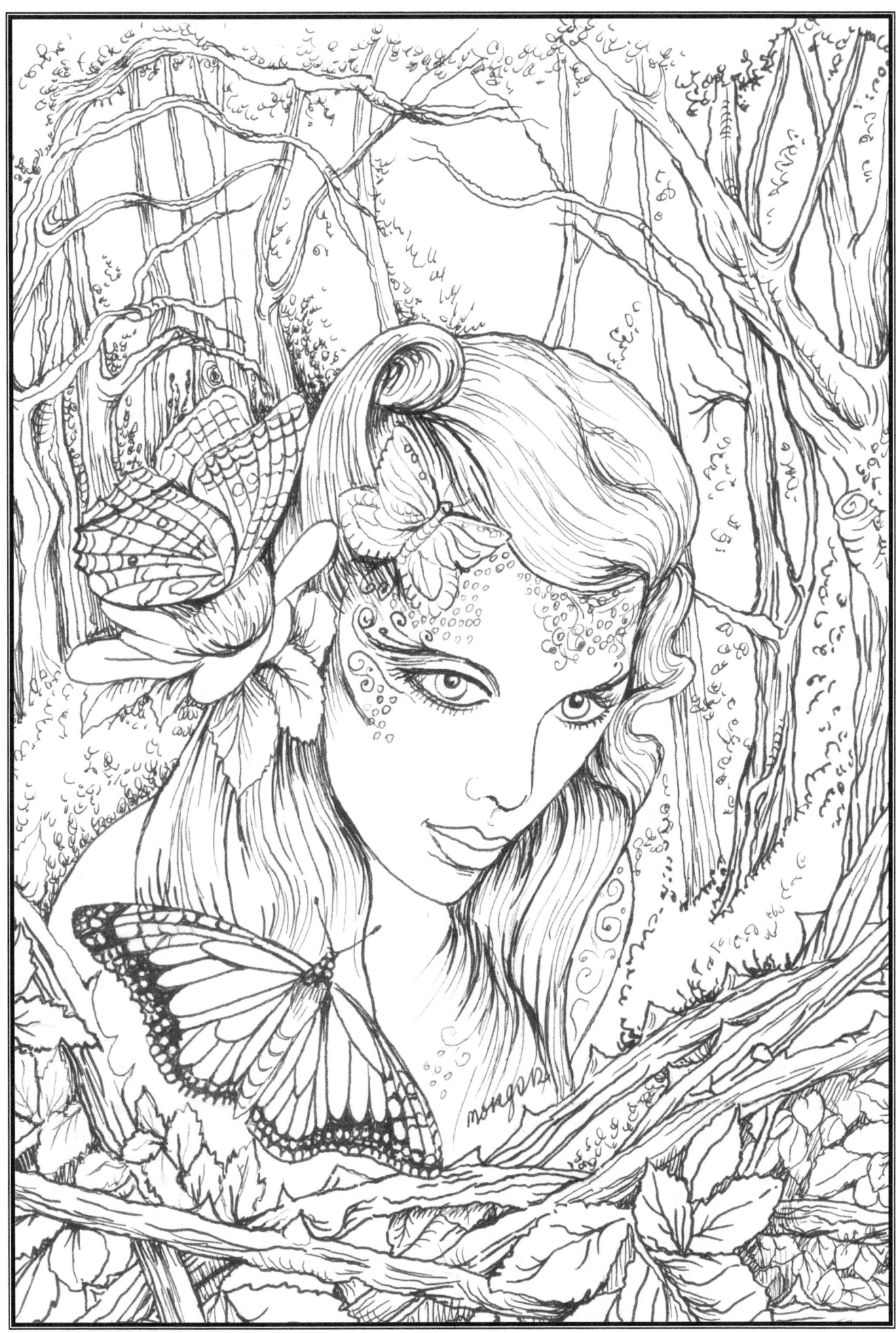

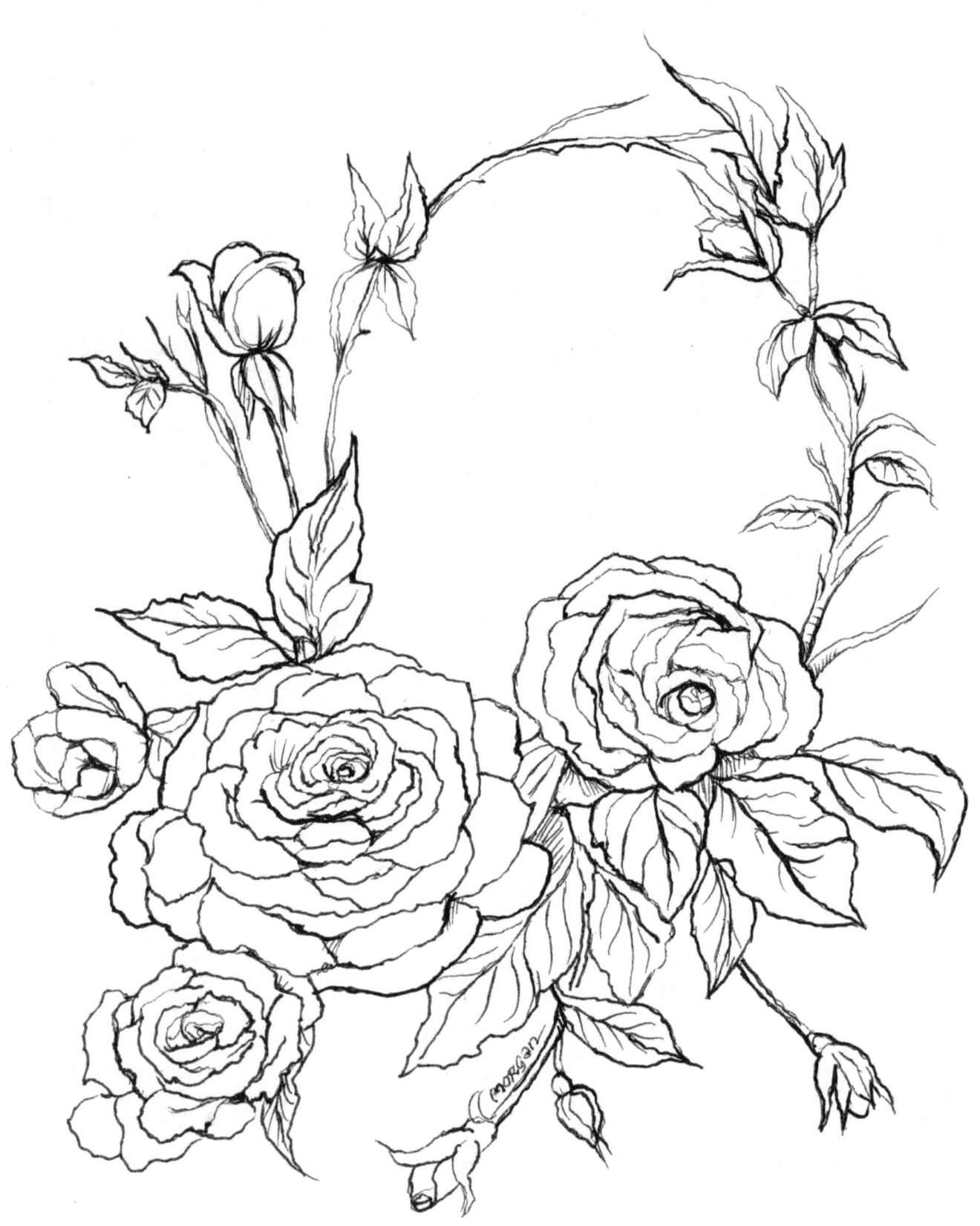

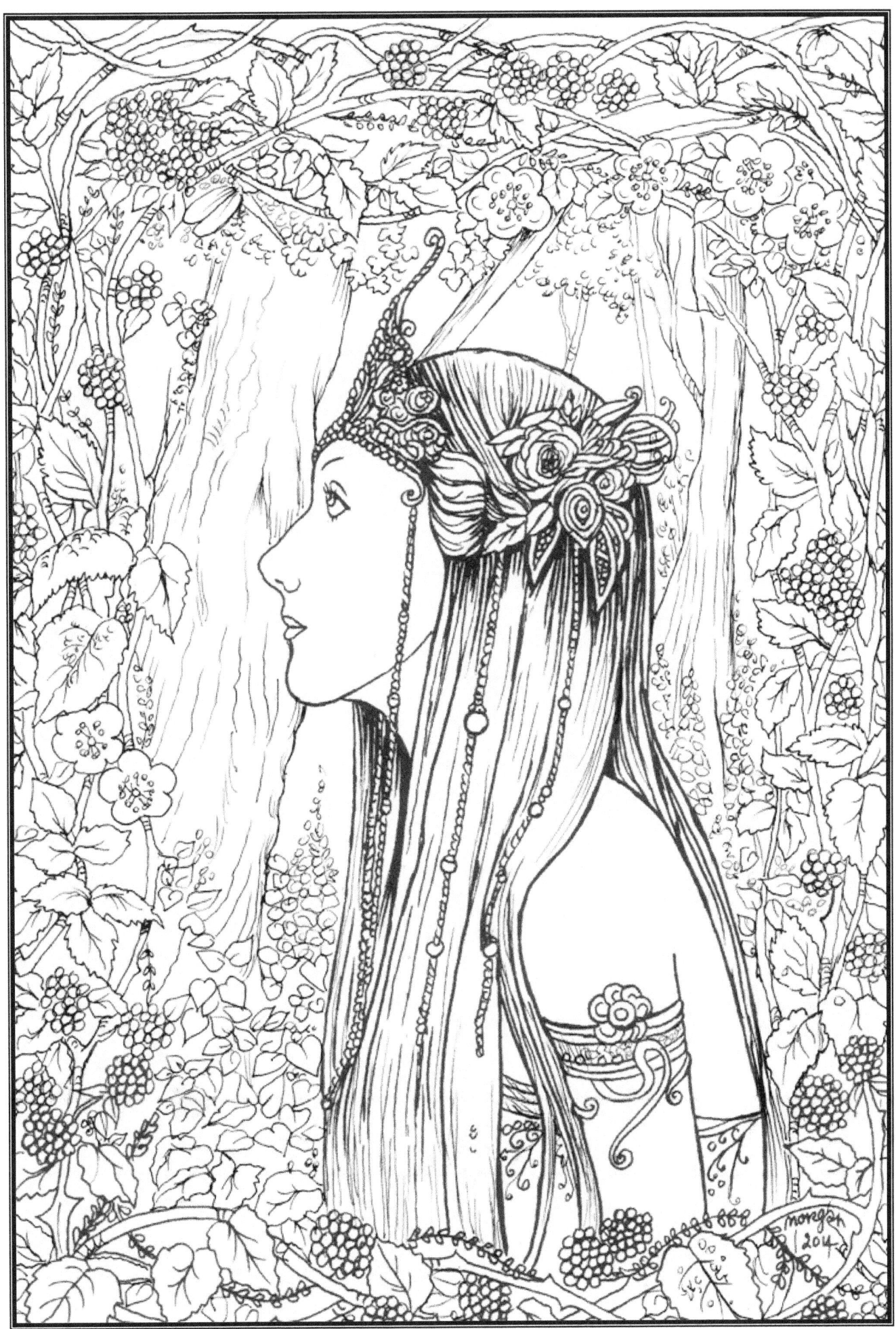

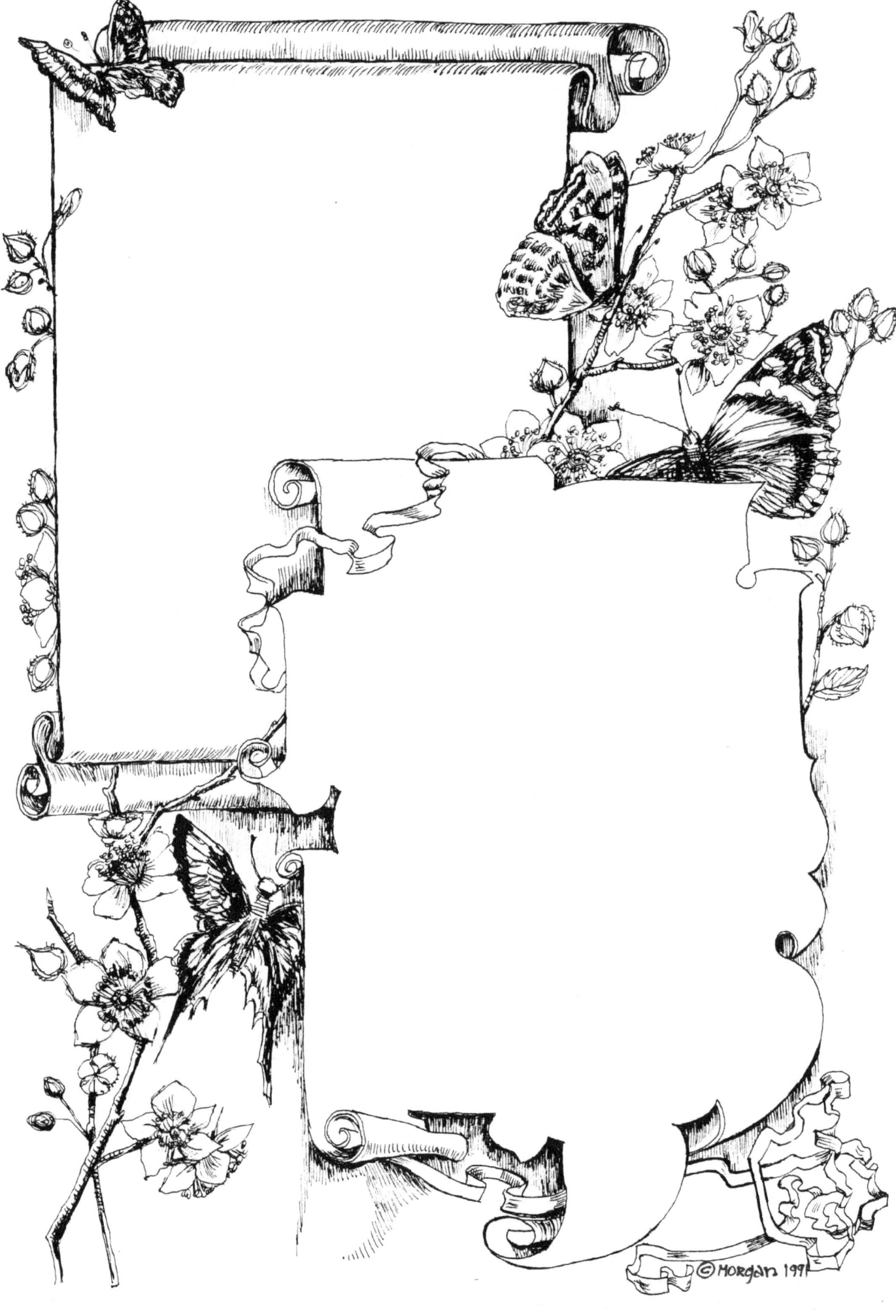

© Morgan 1991

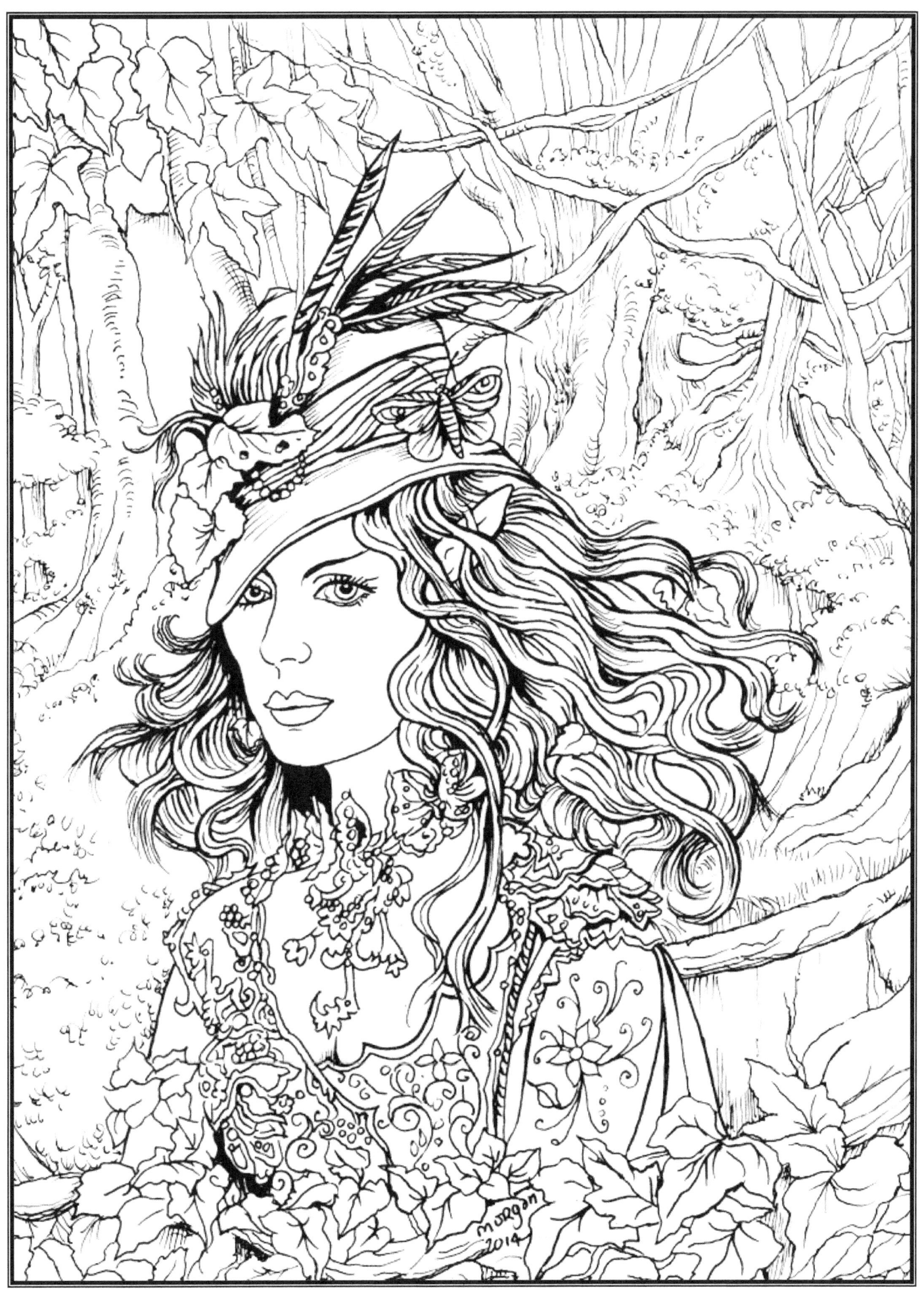

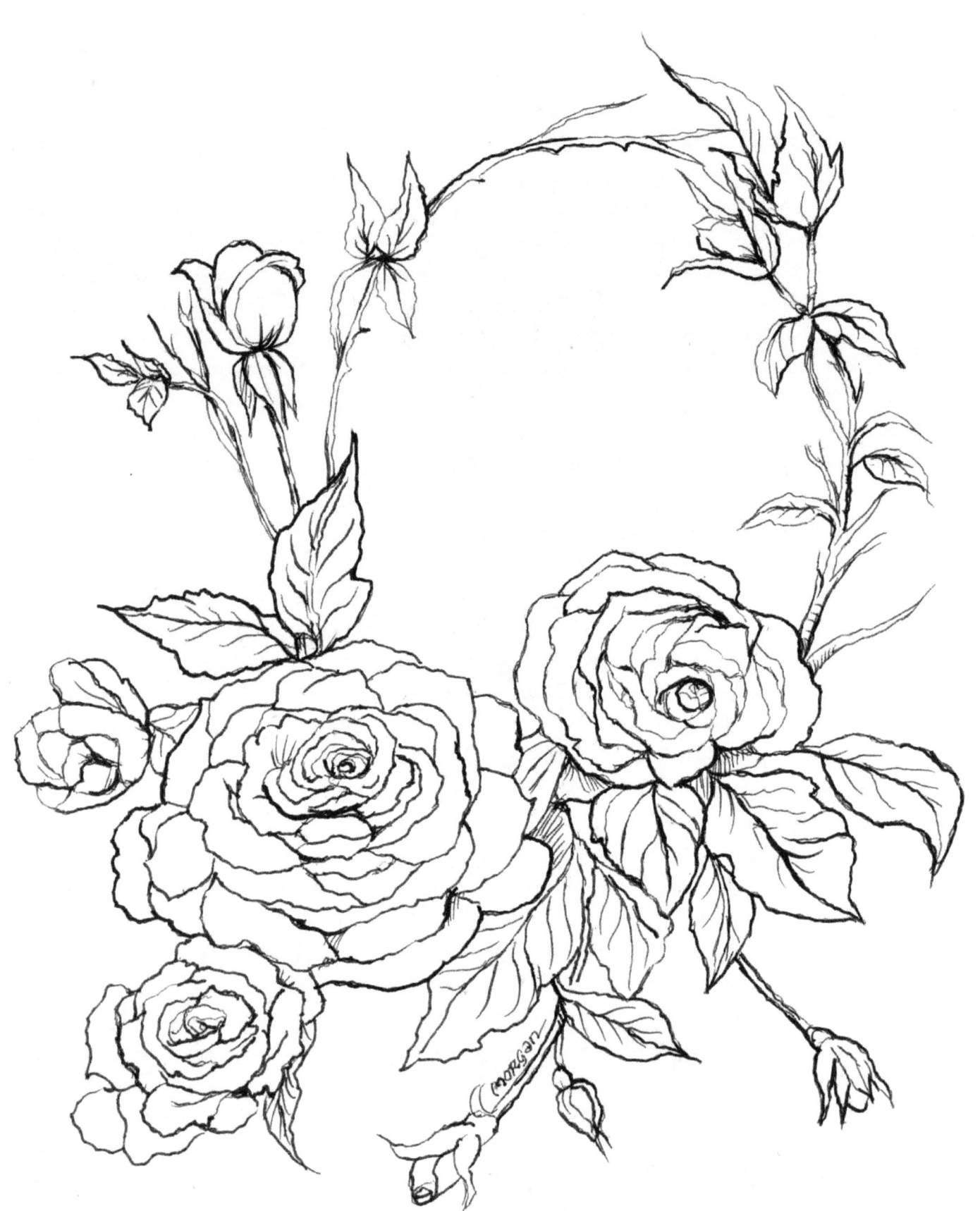

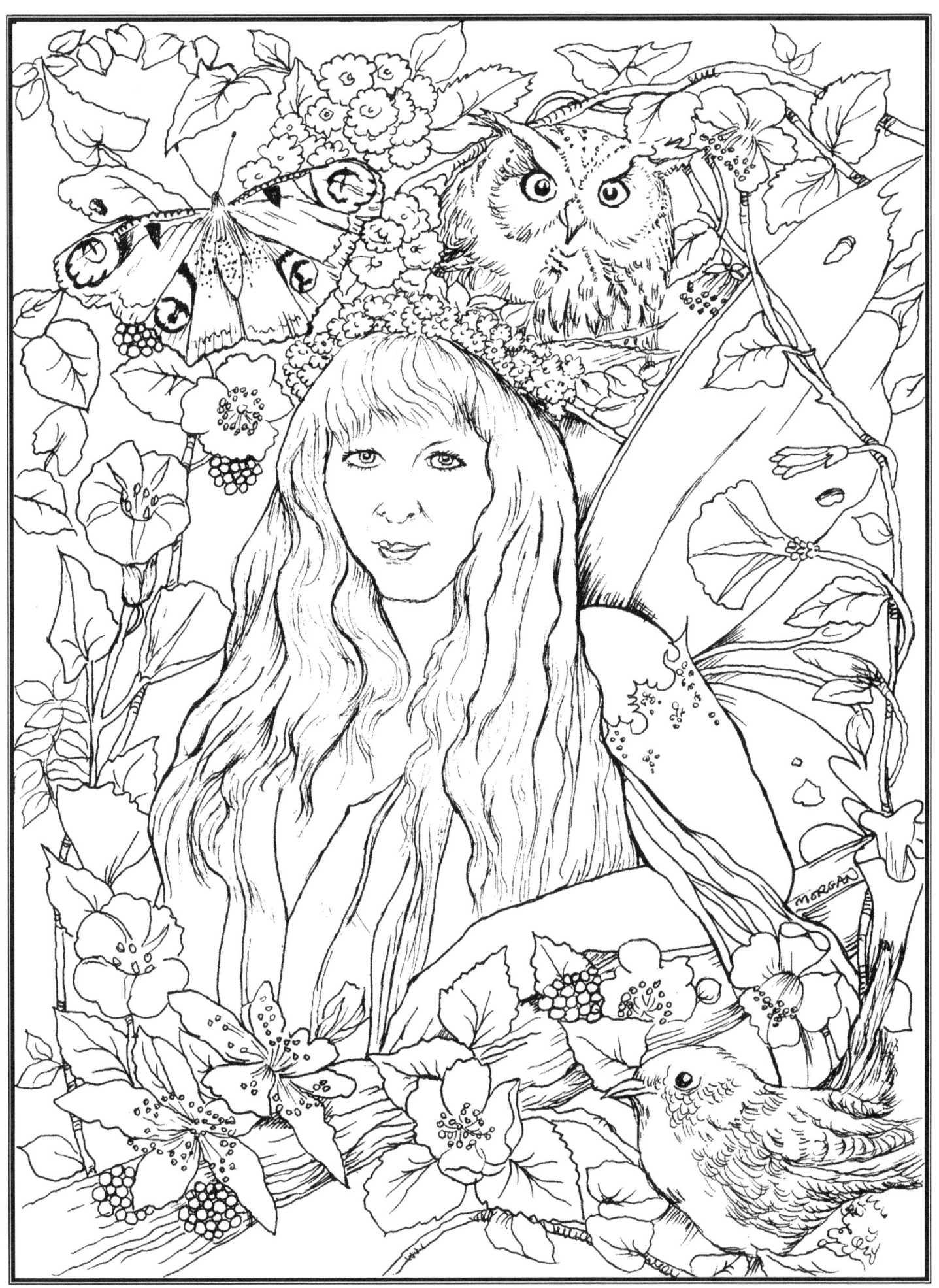

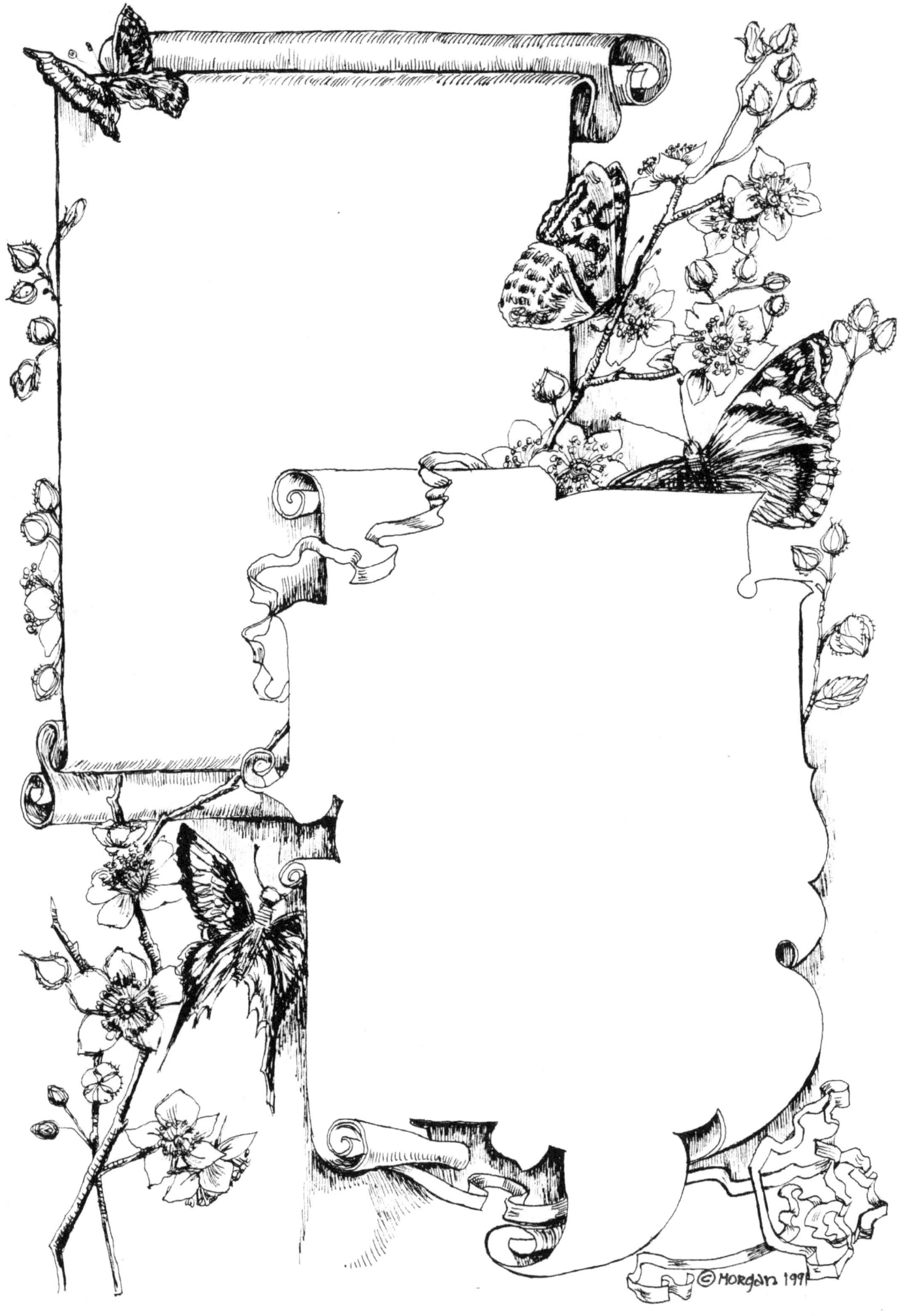

© Morgan 1991

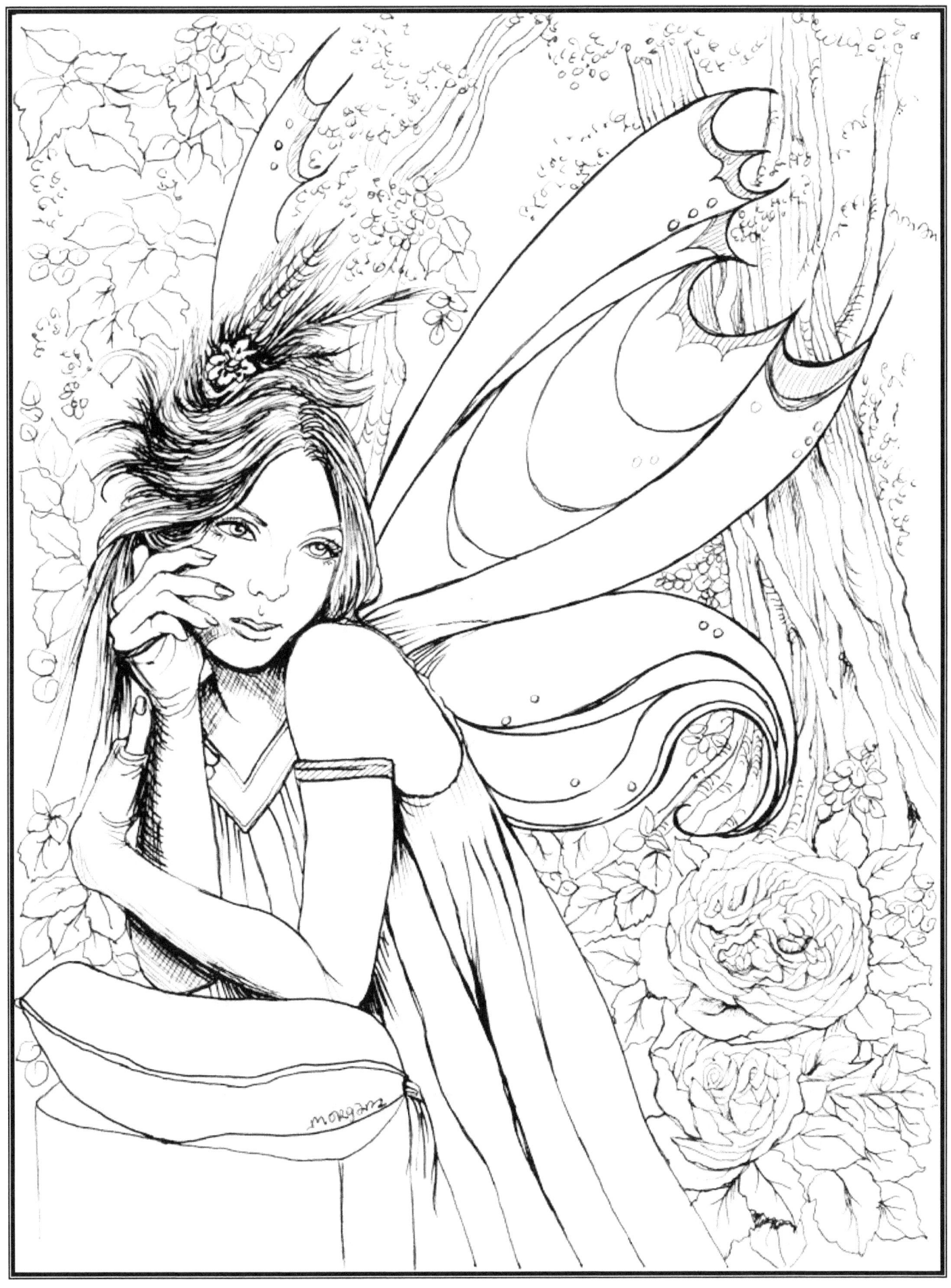

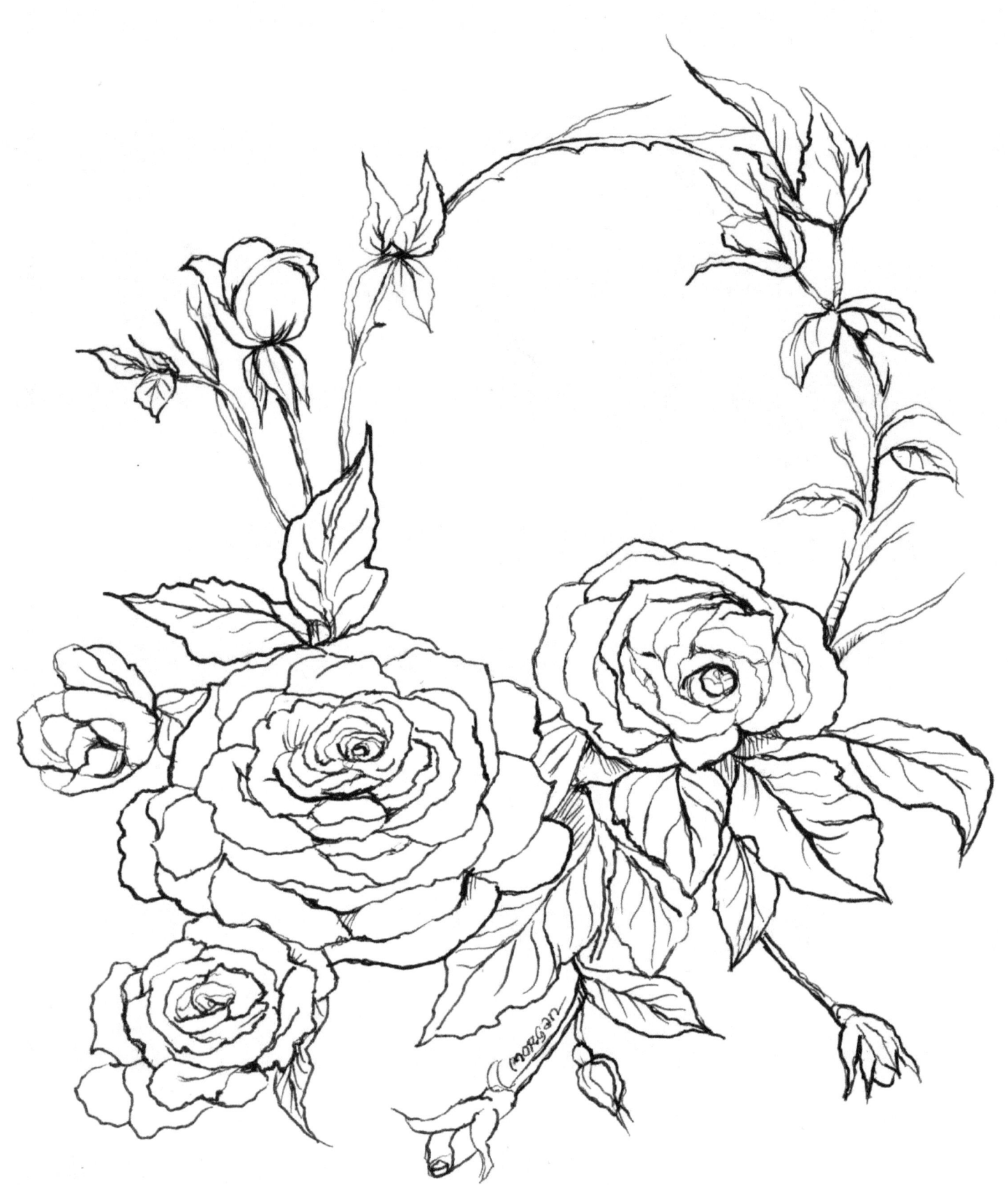

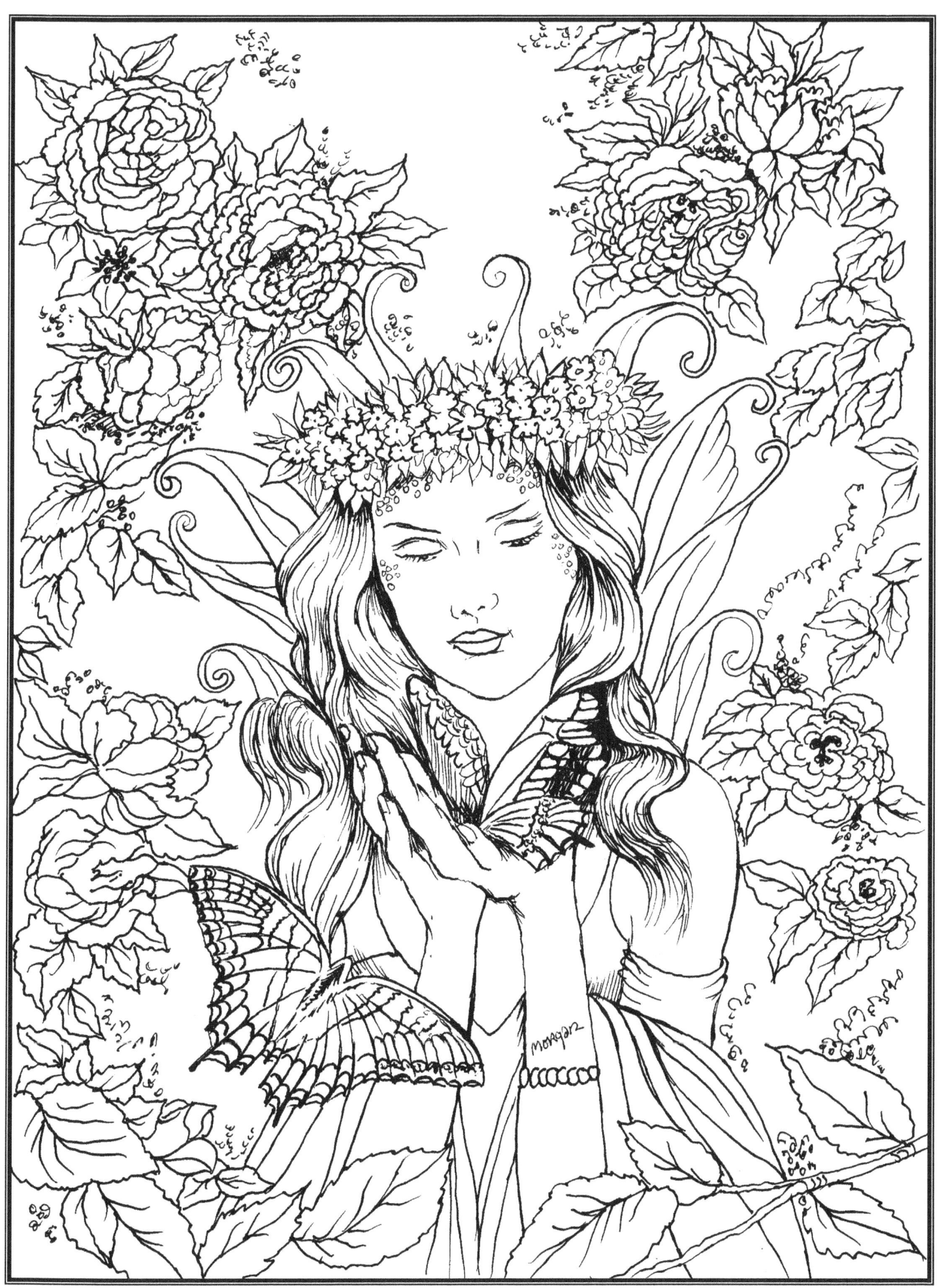

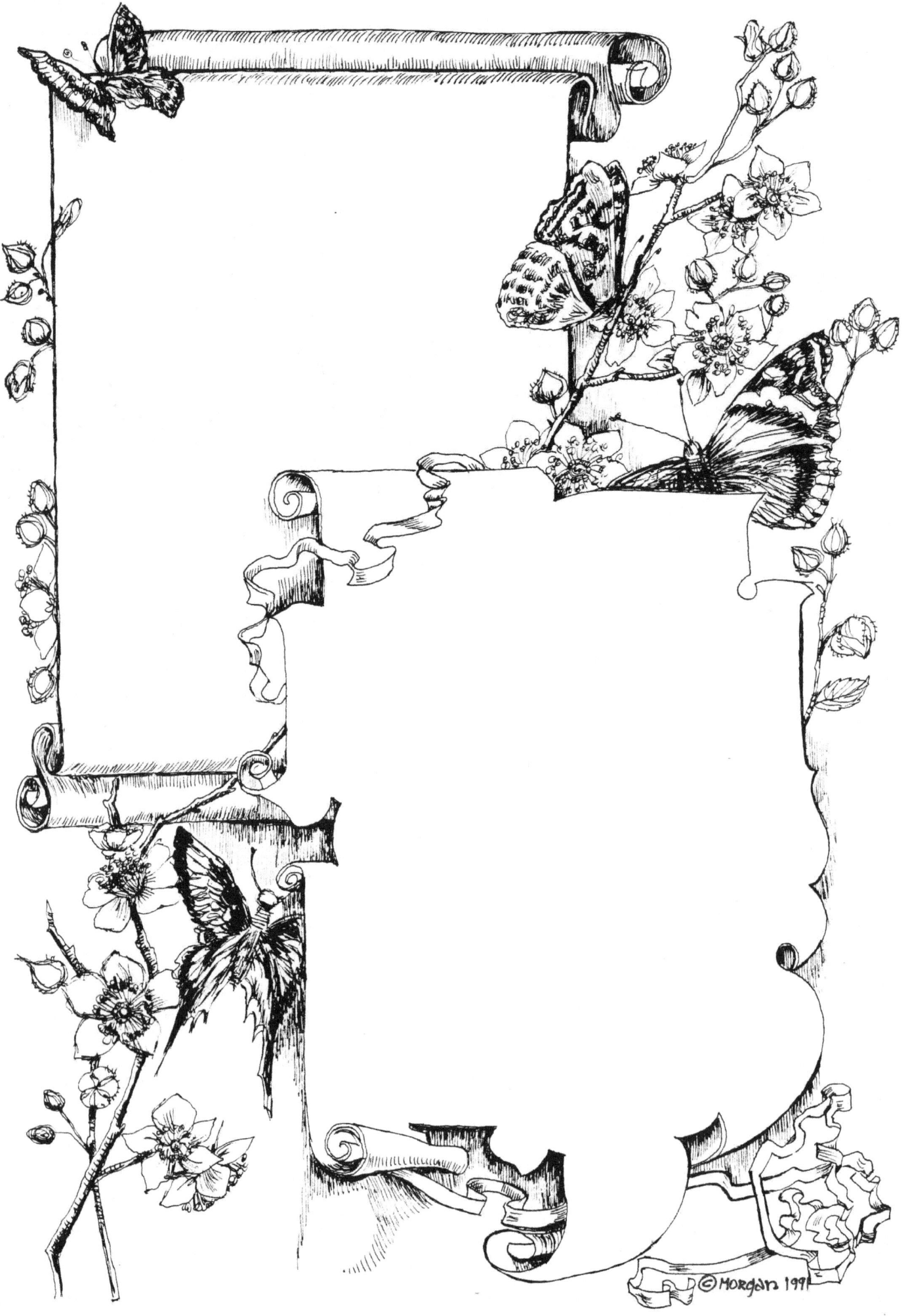

© Morgan 1991

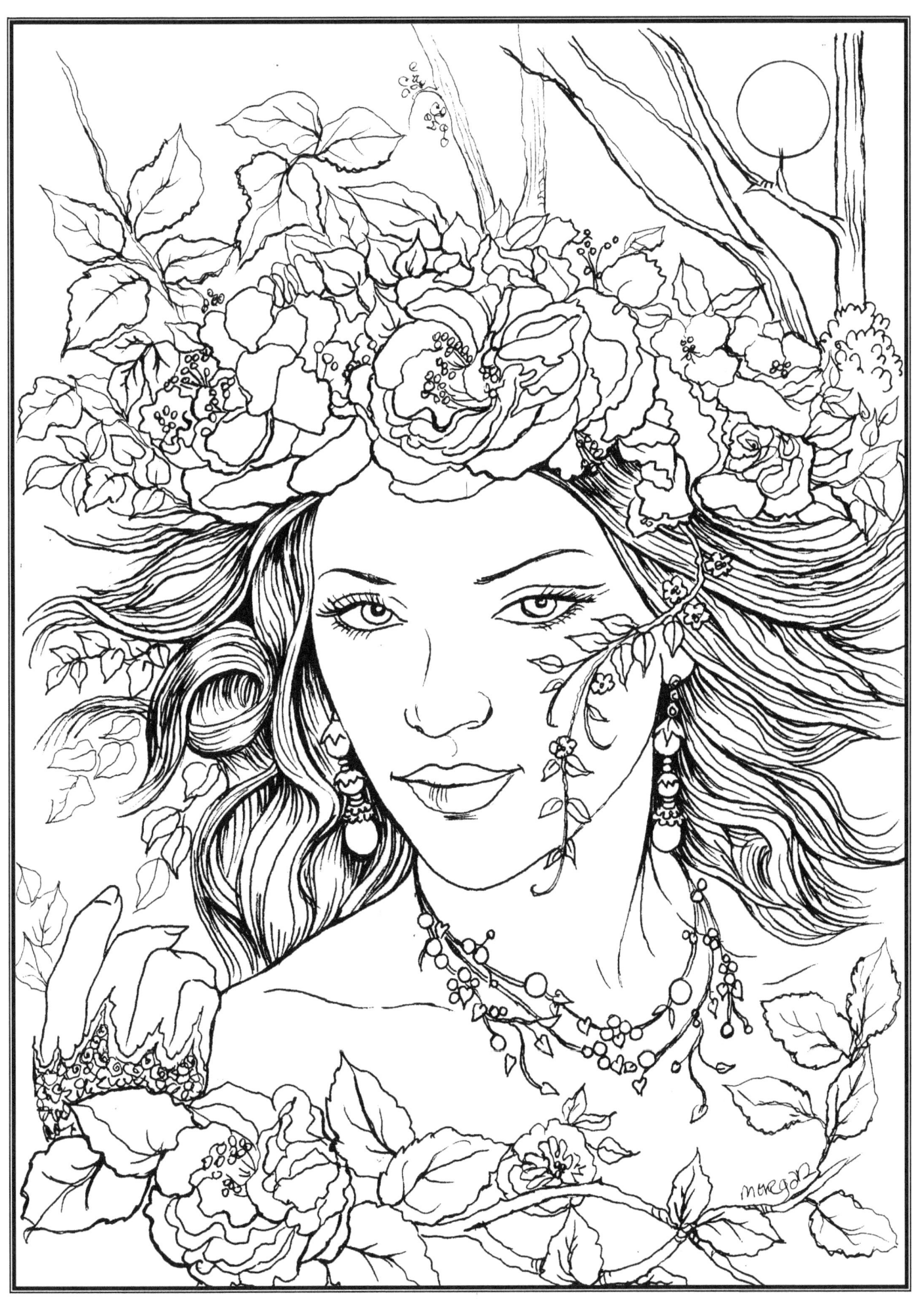

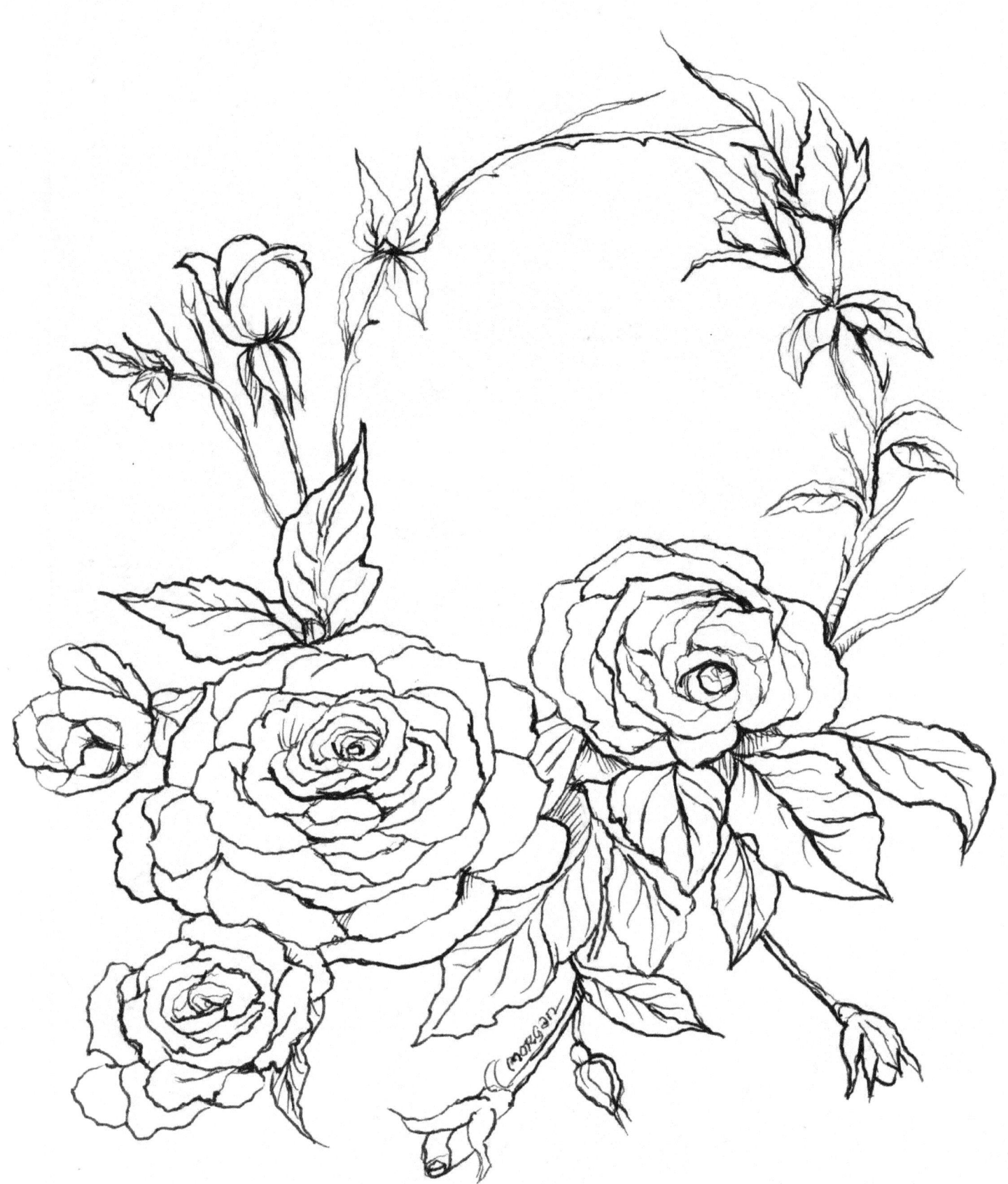

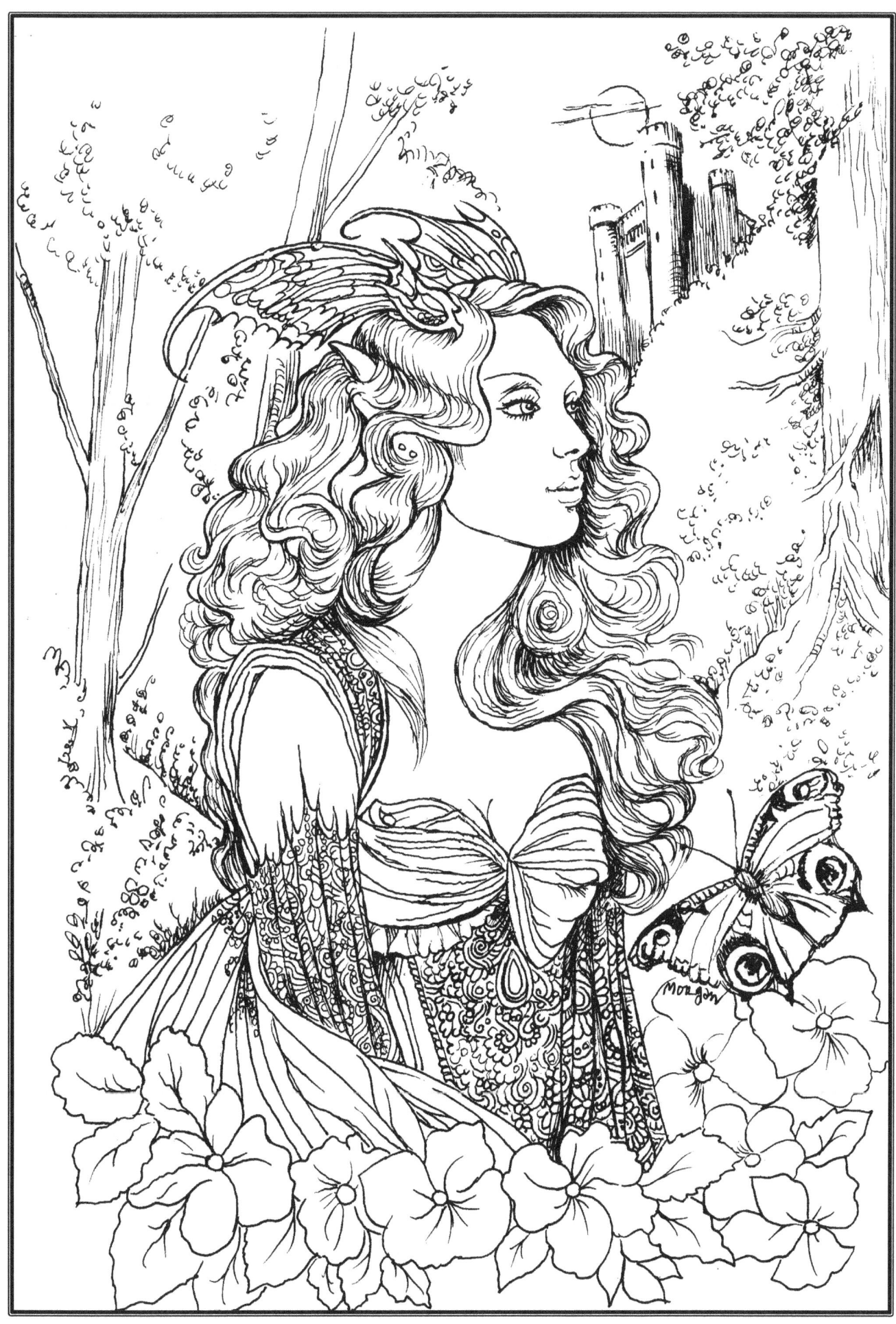

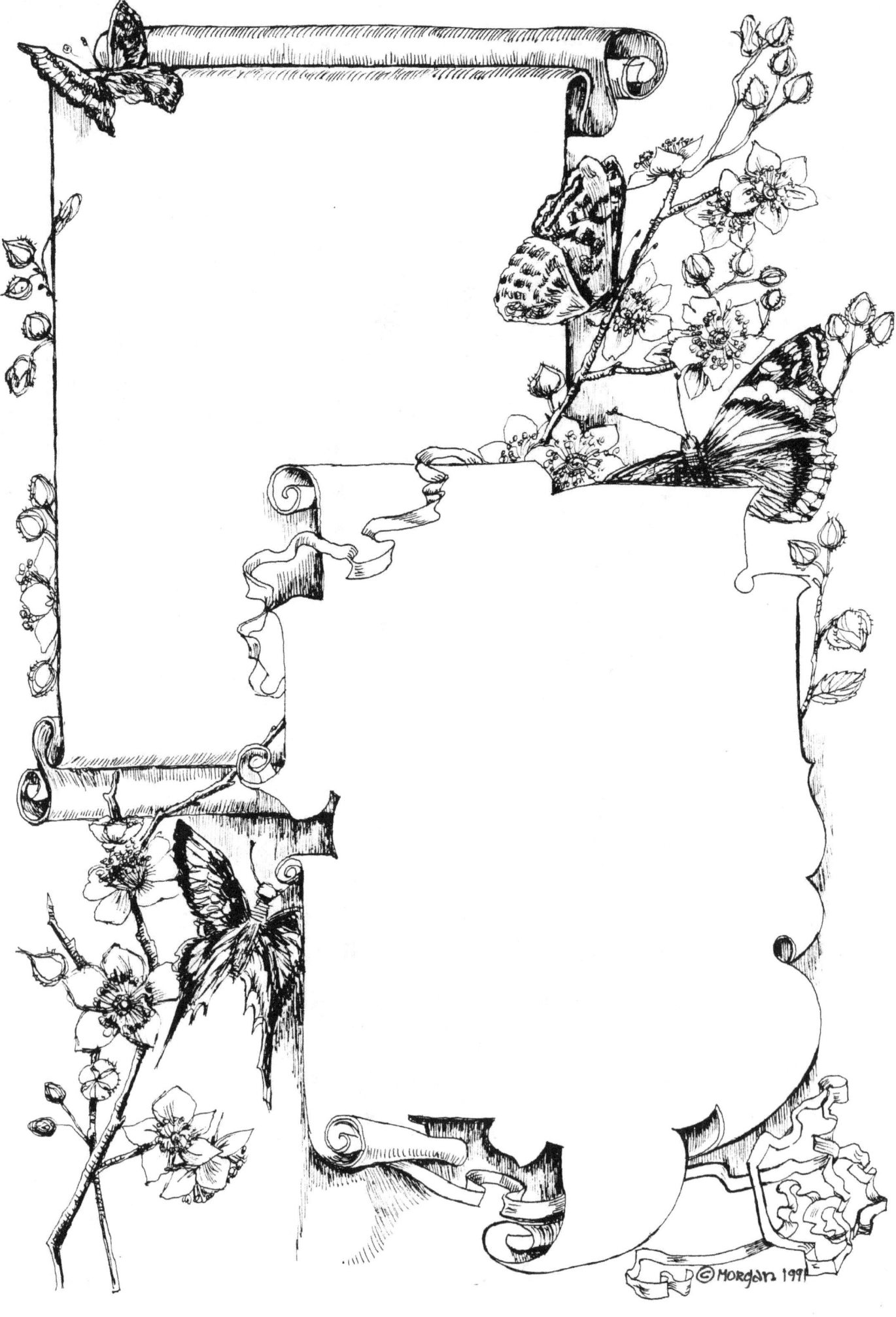

© Morgan 1991

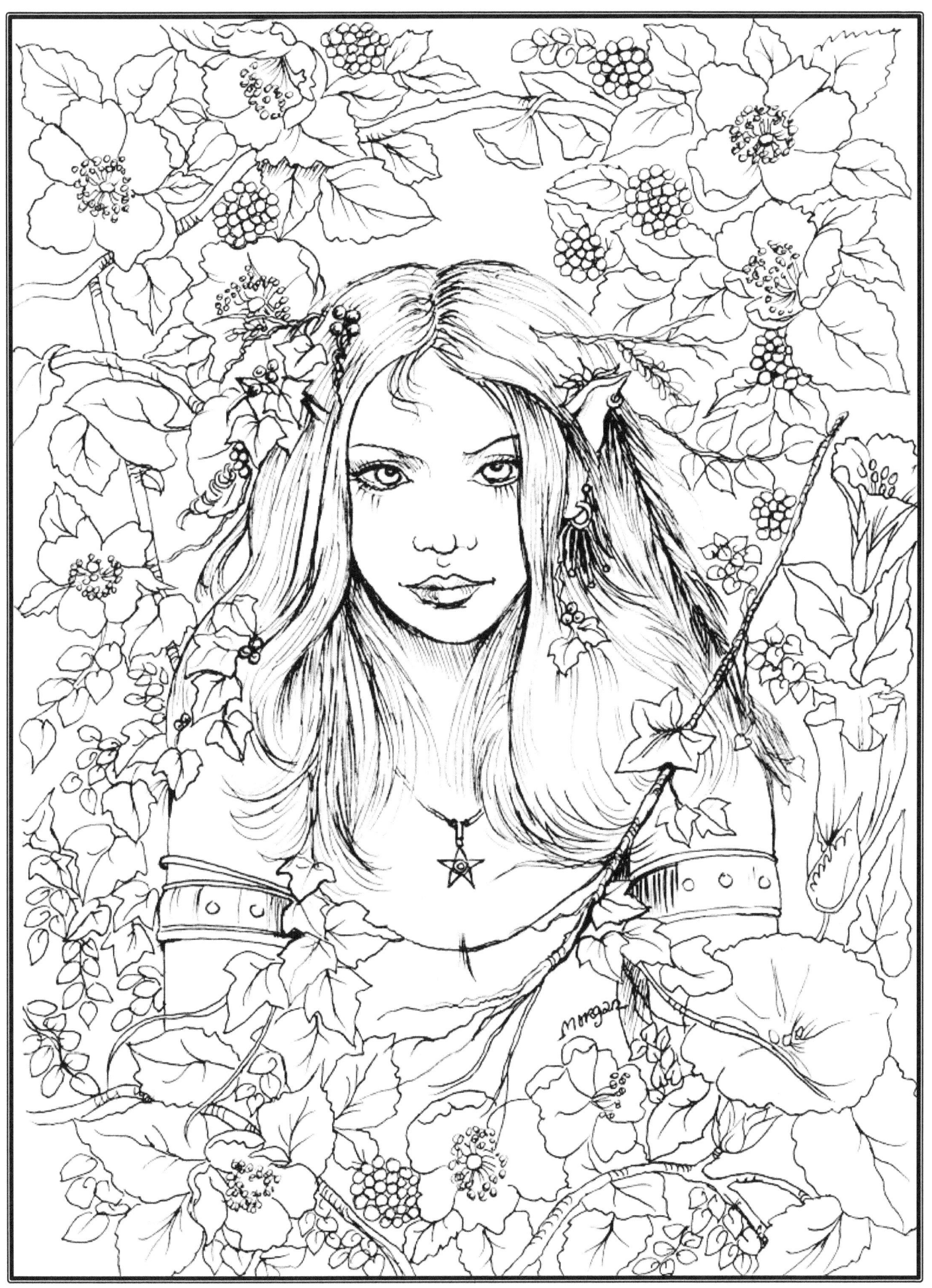

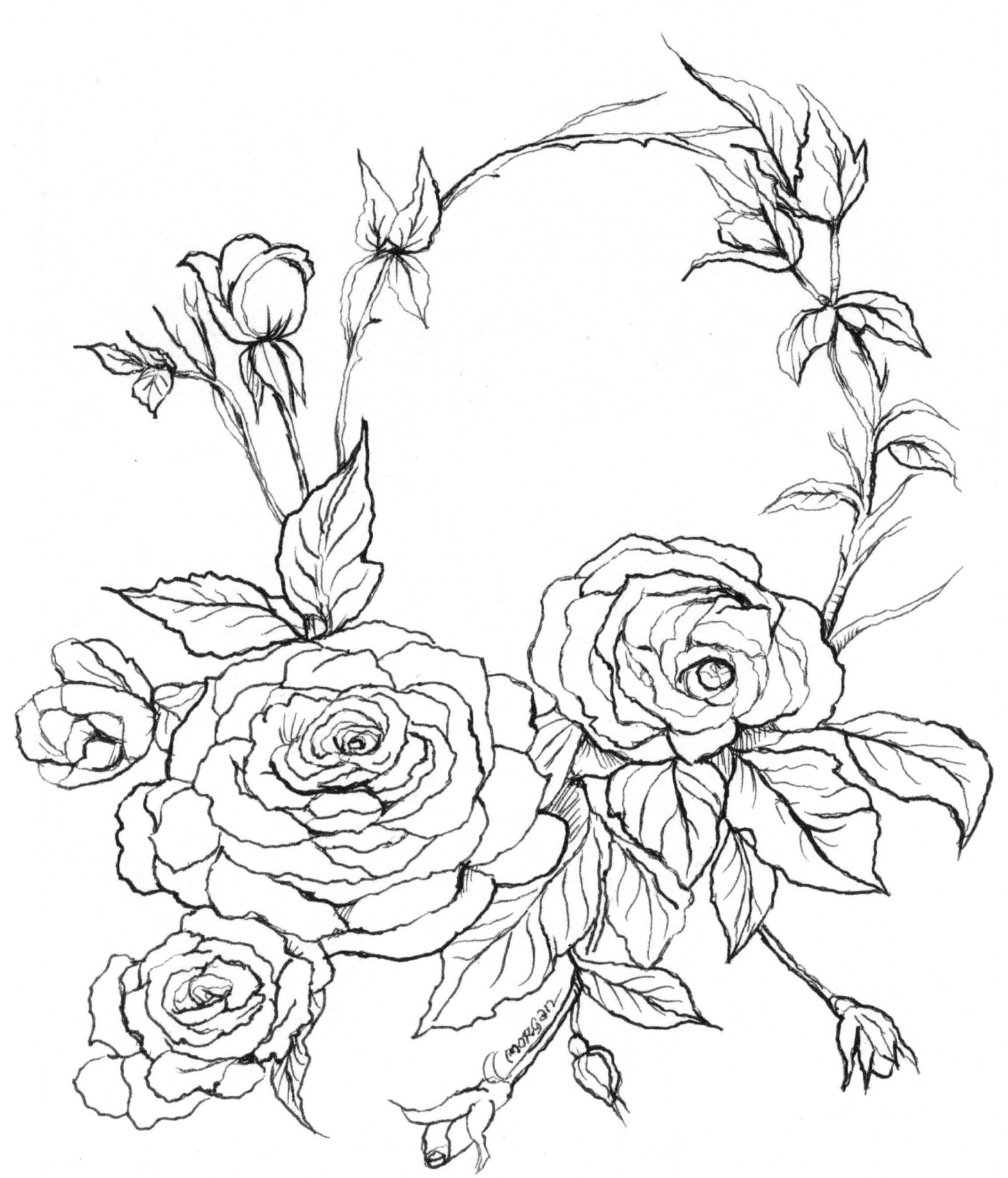

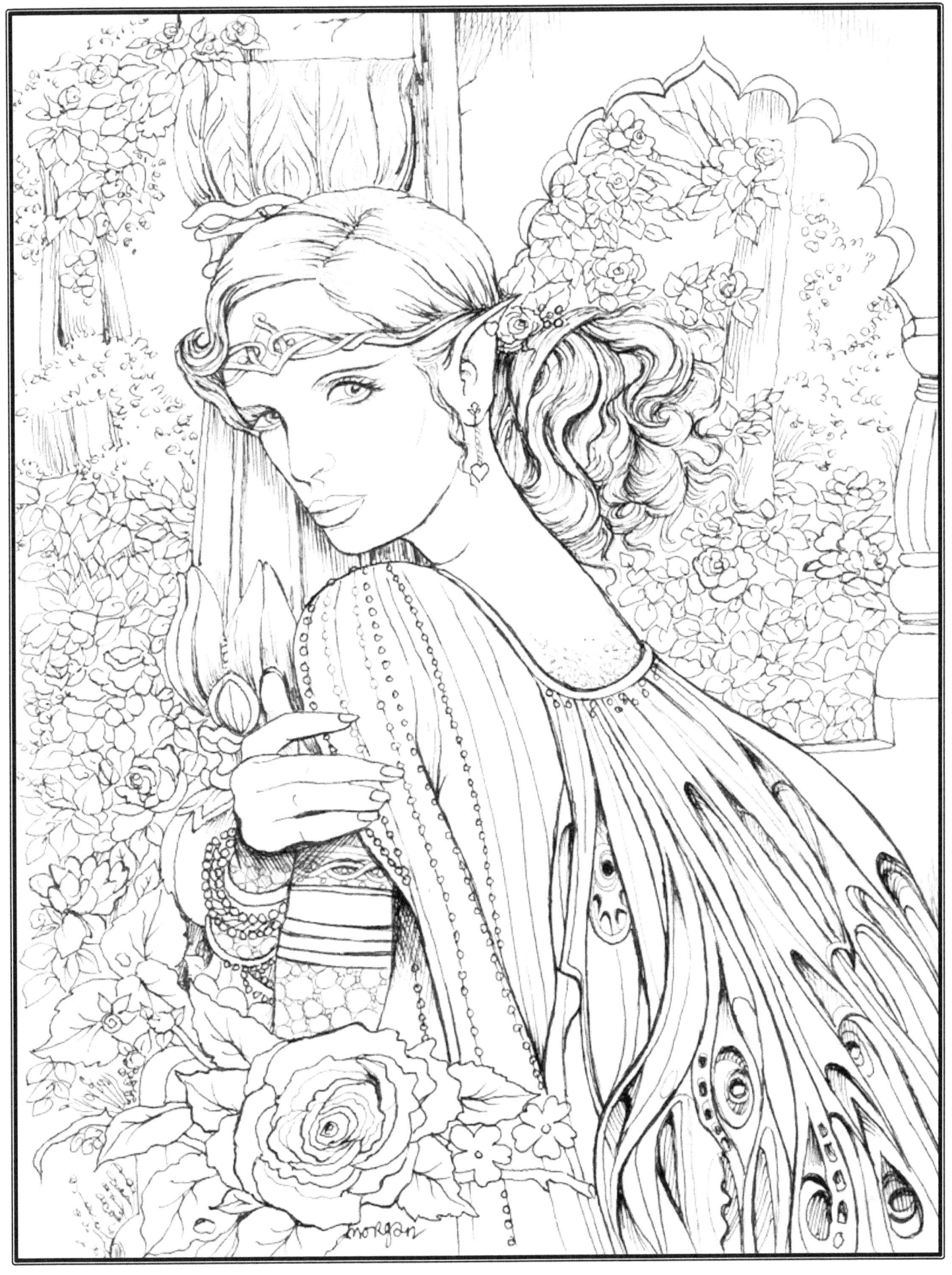

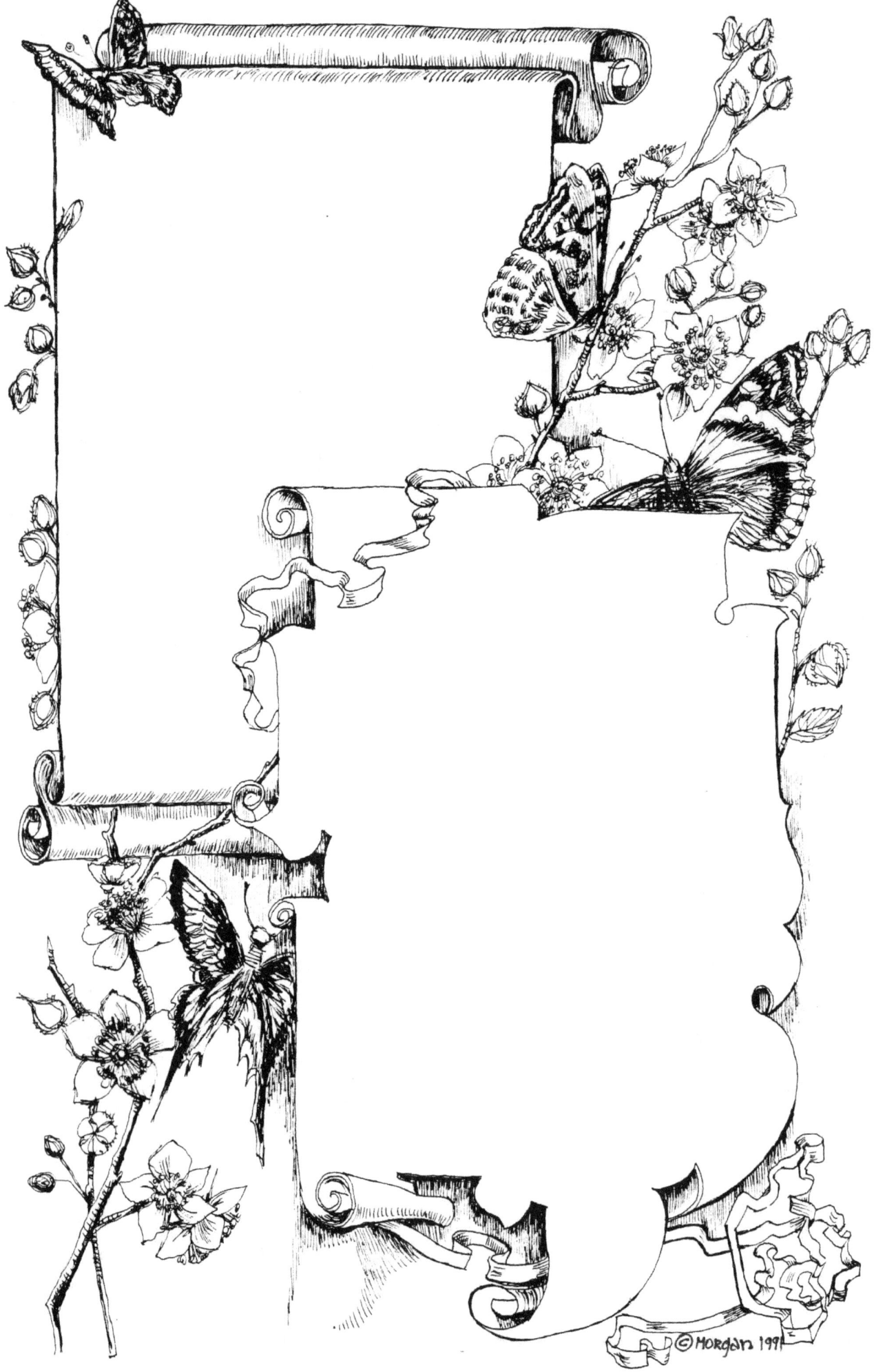

© Morgan 1991

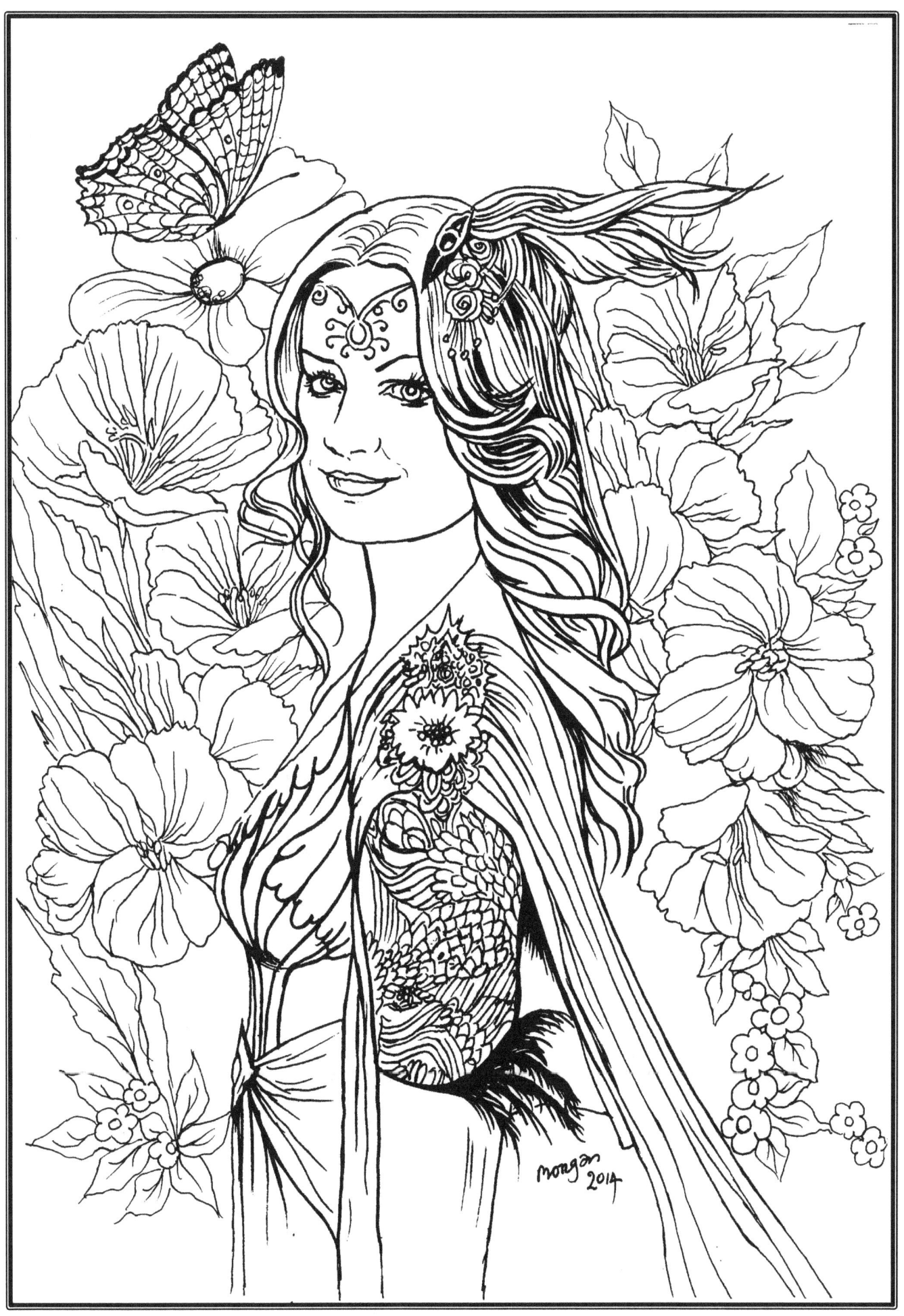

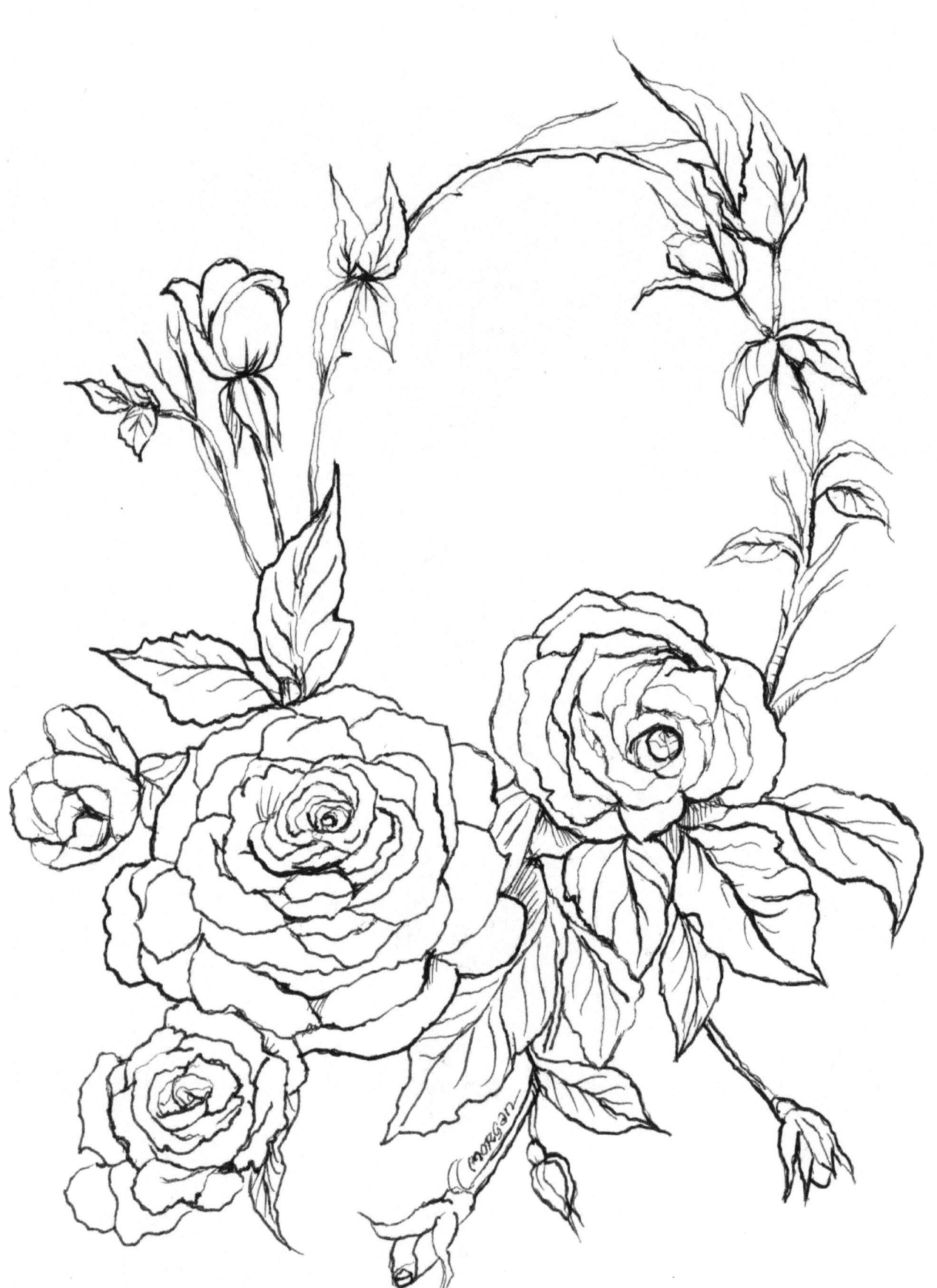

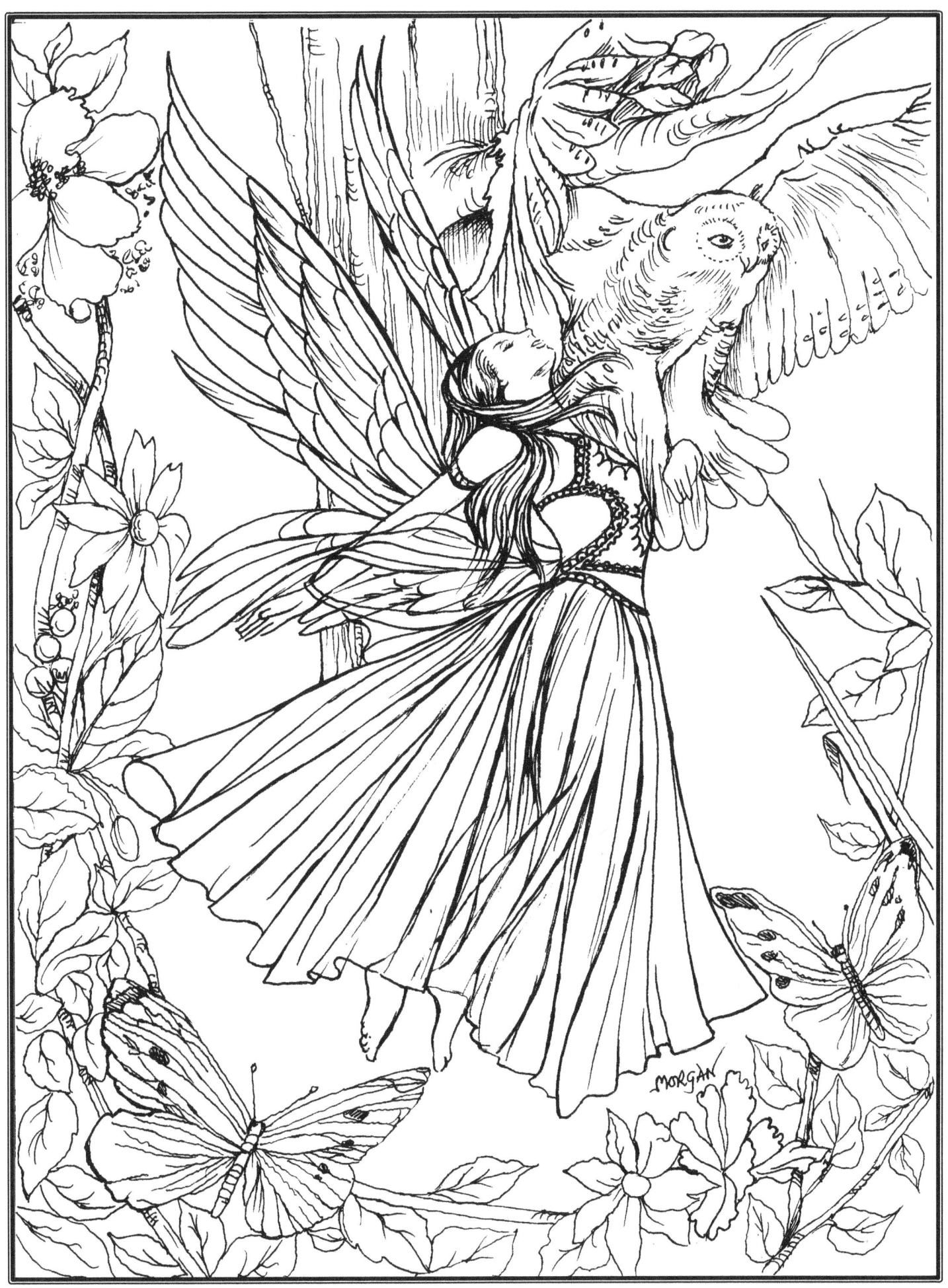

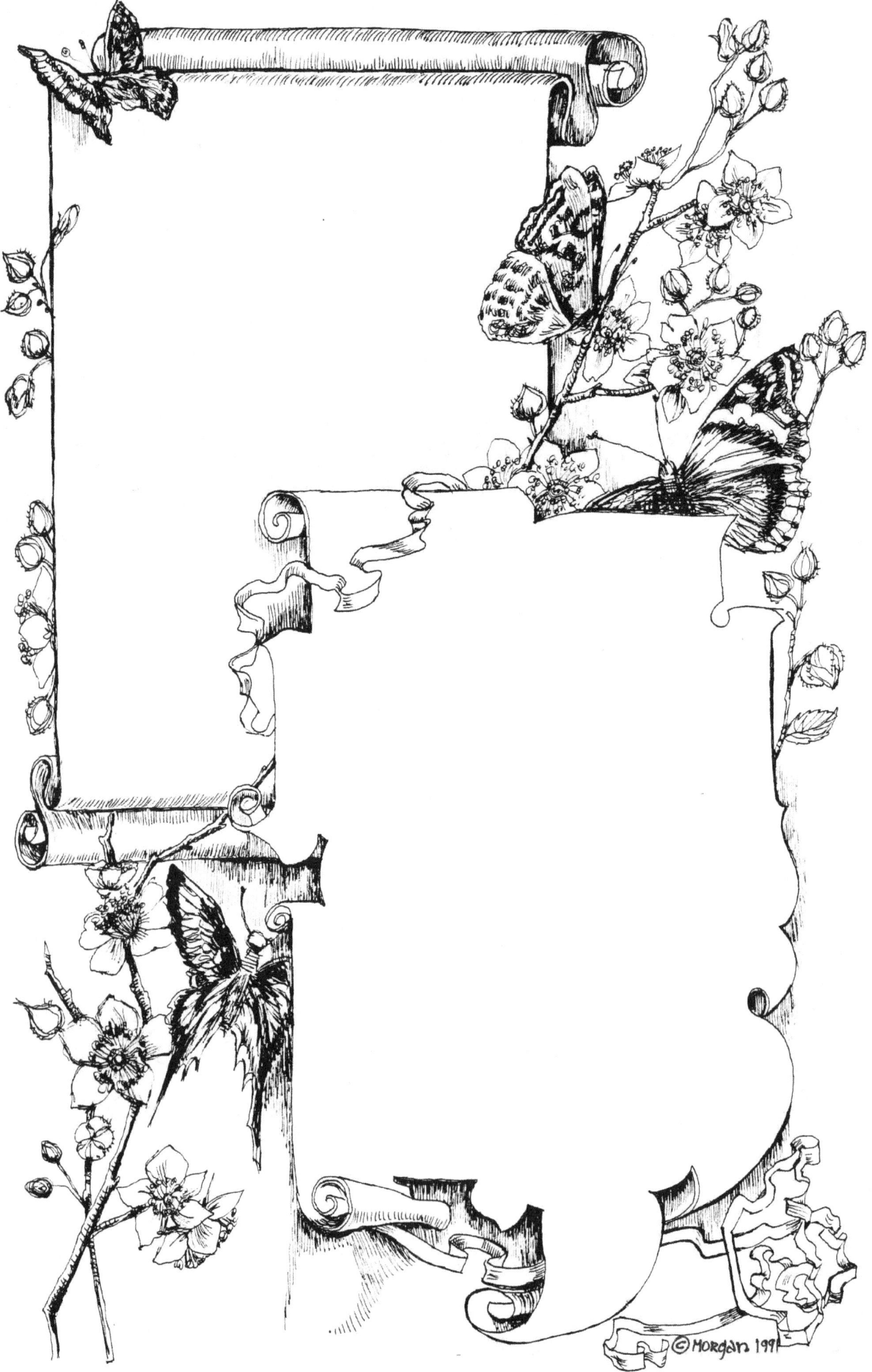

©Morgan 1991

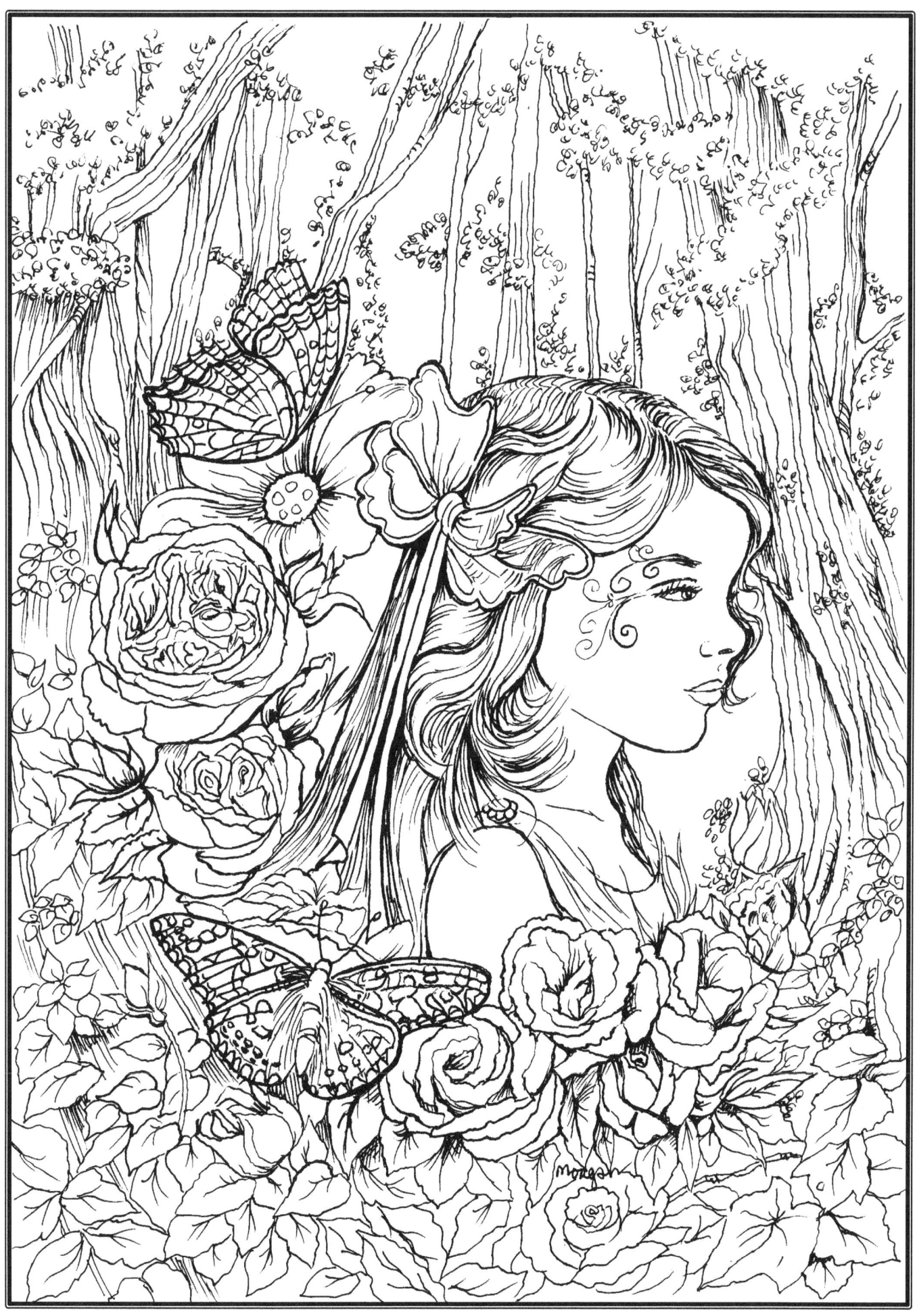

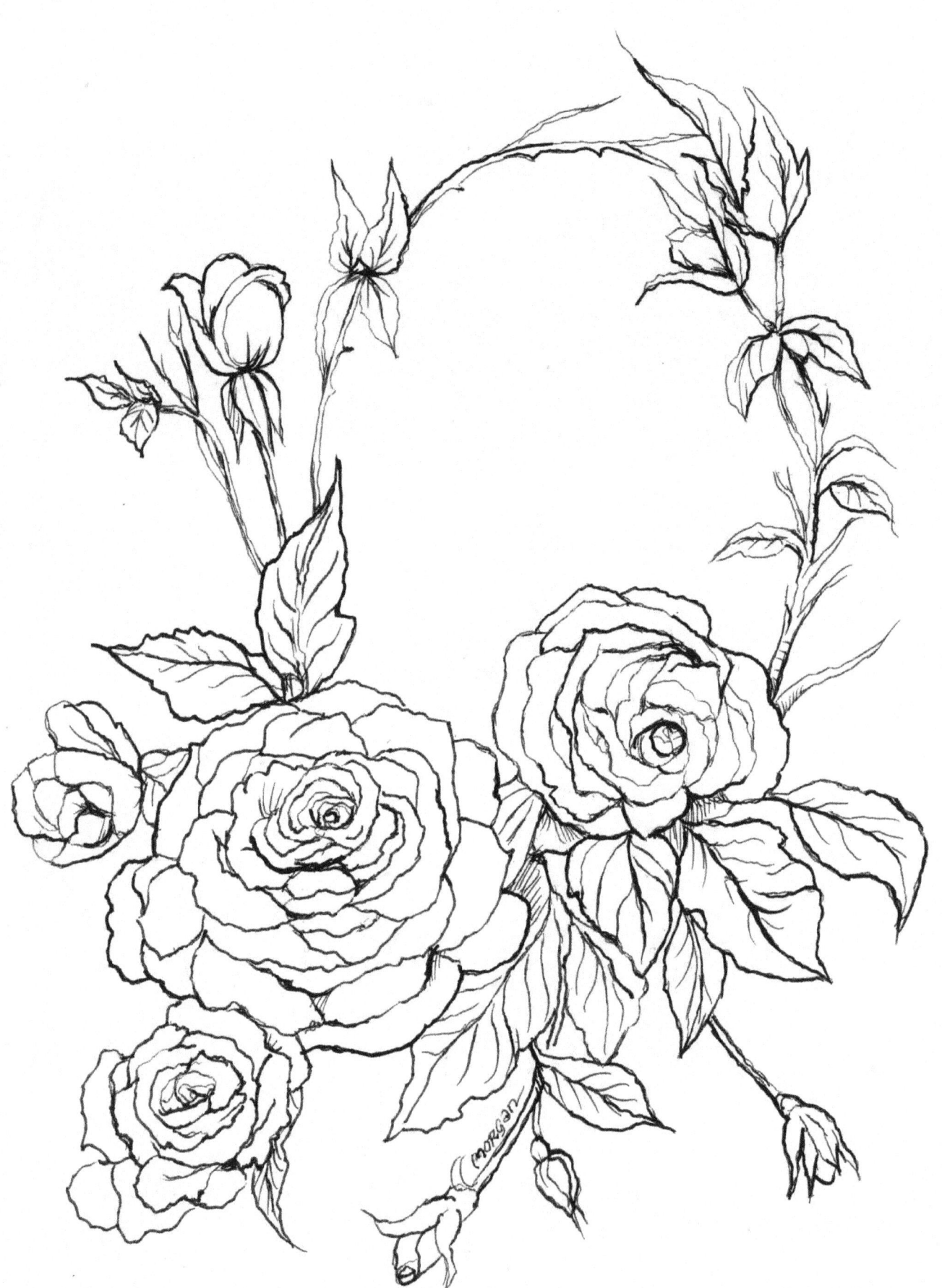

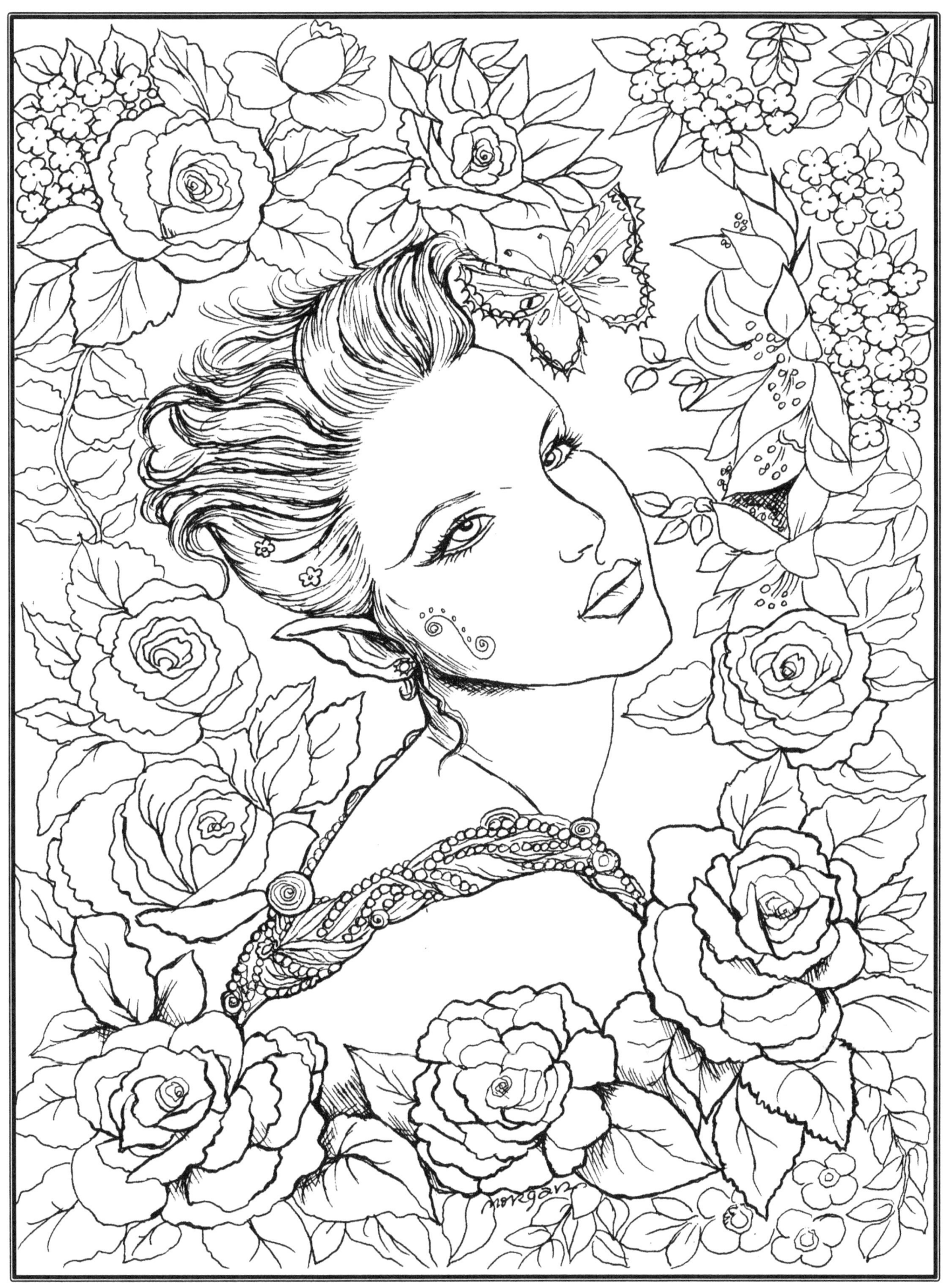

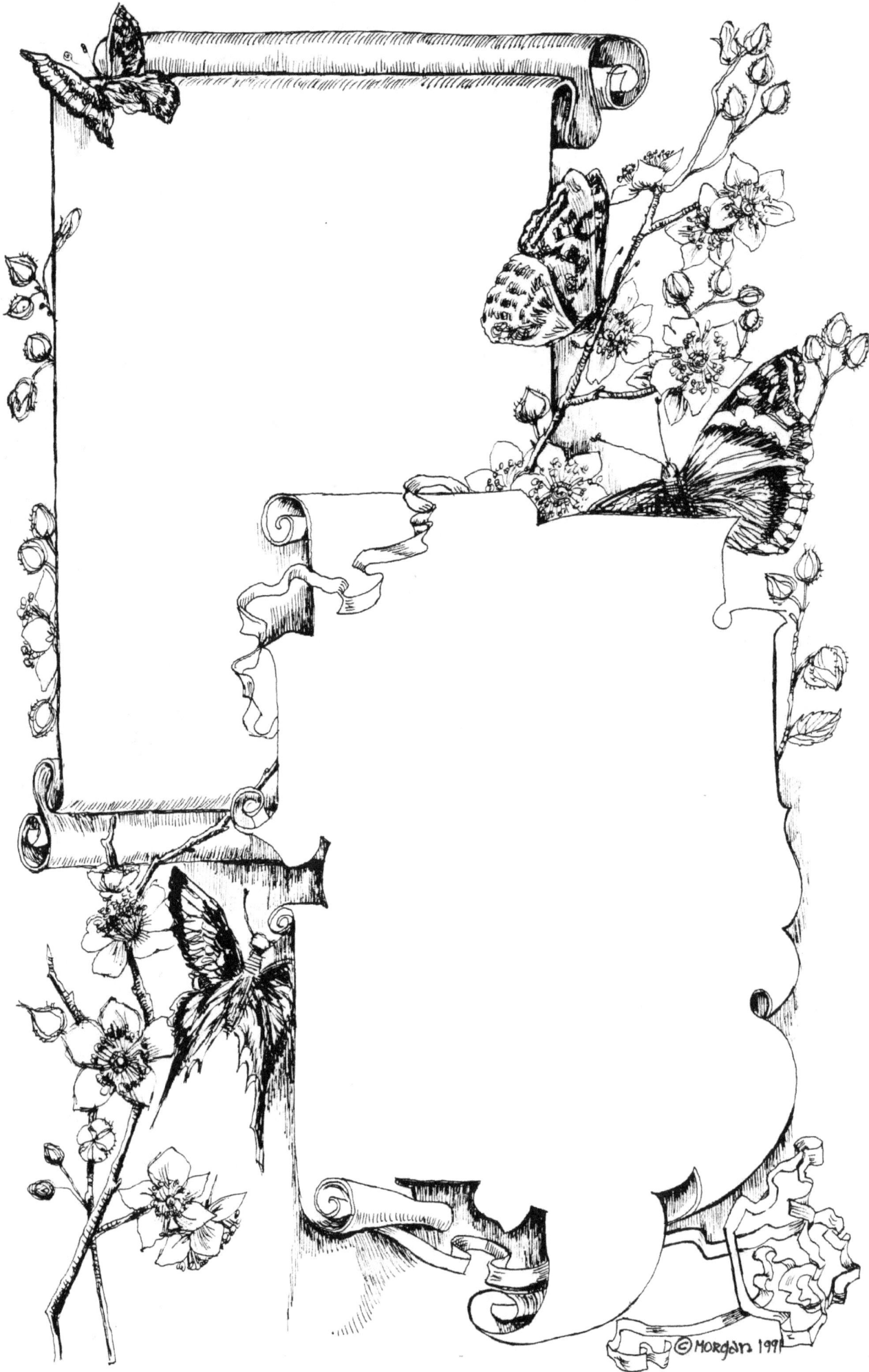

© Morgan 1991

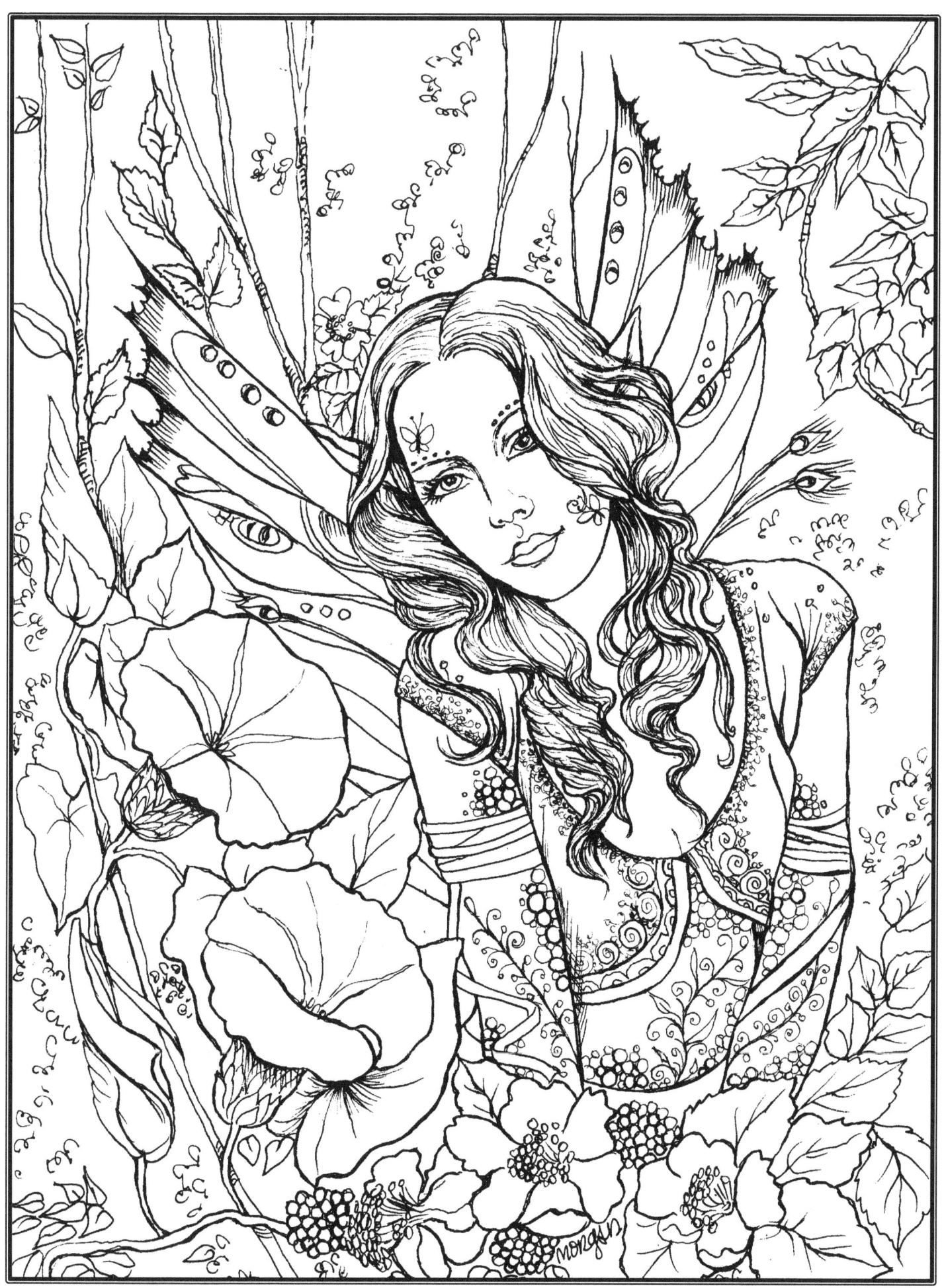

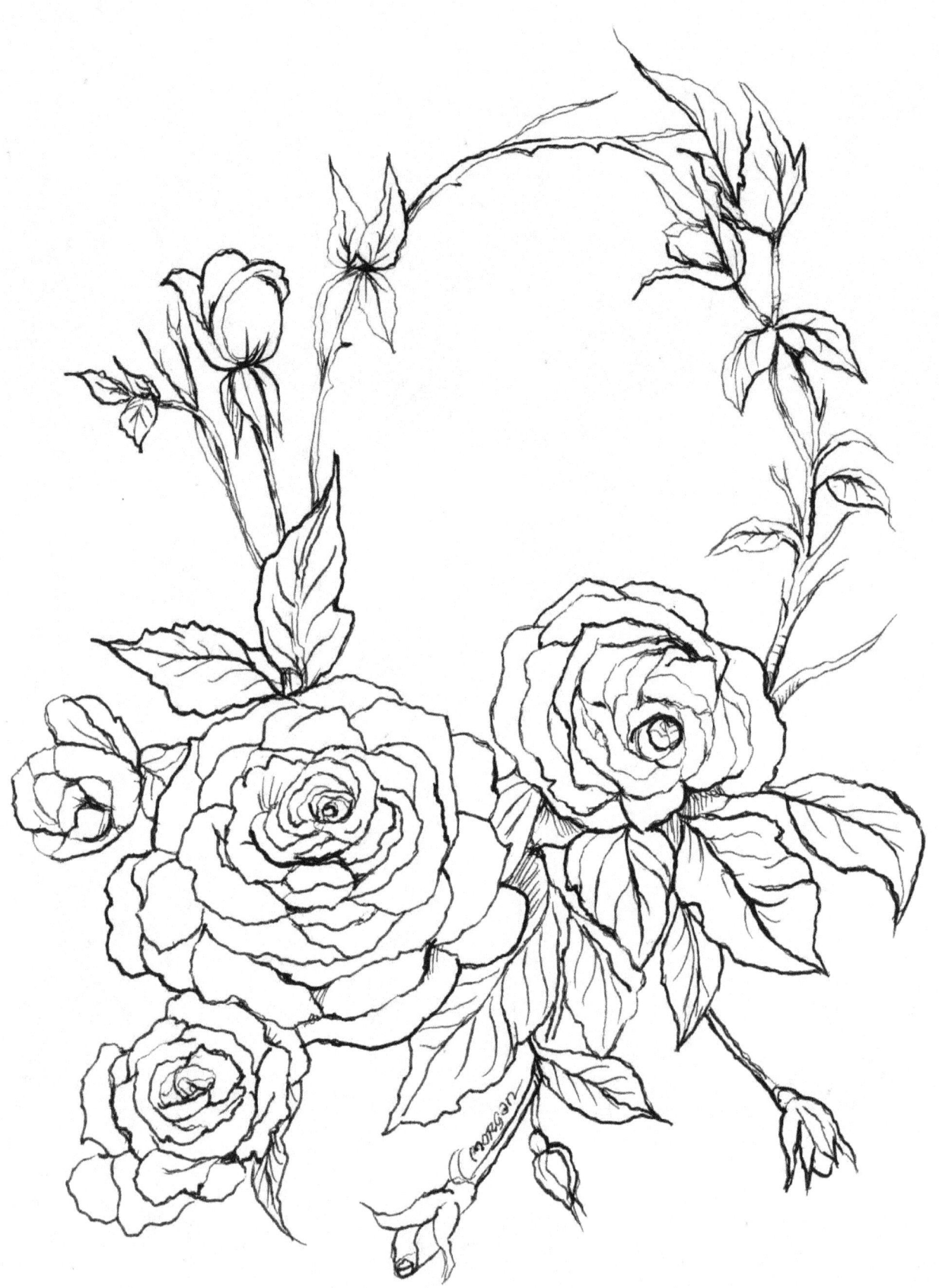

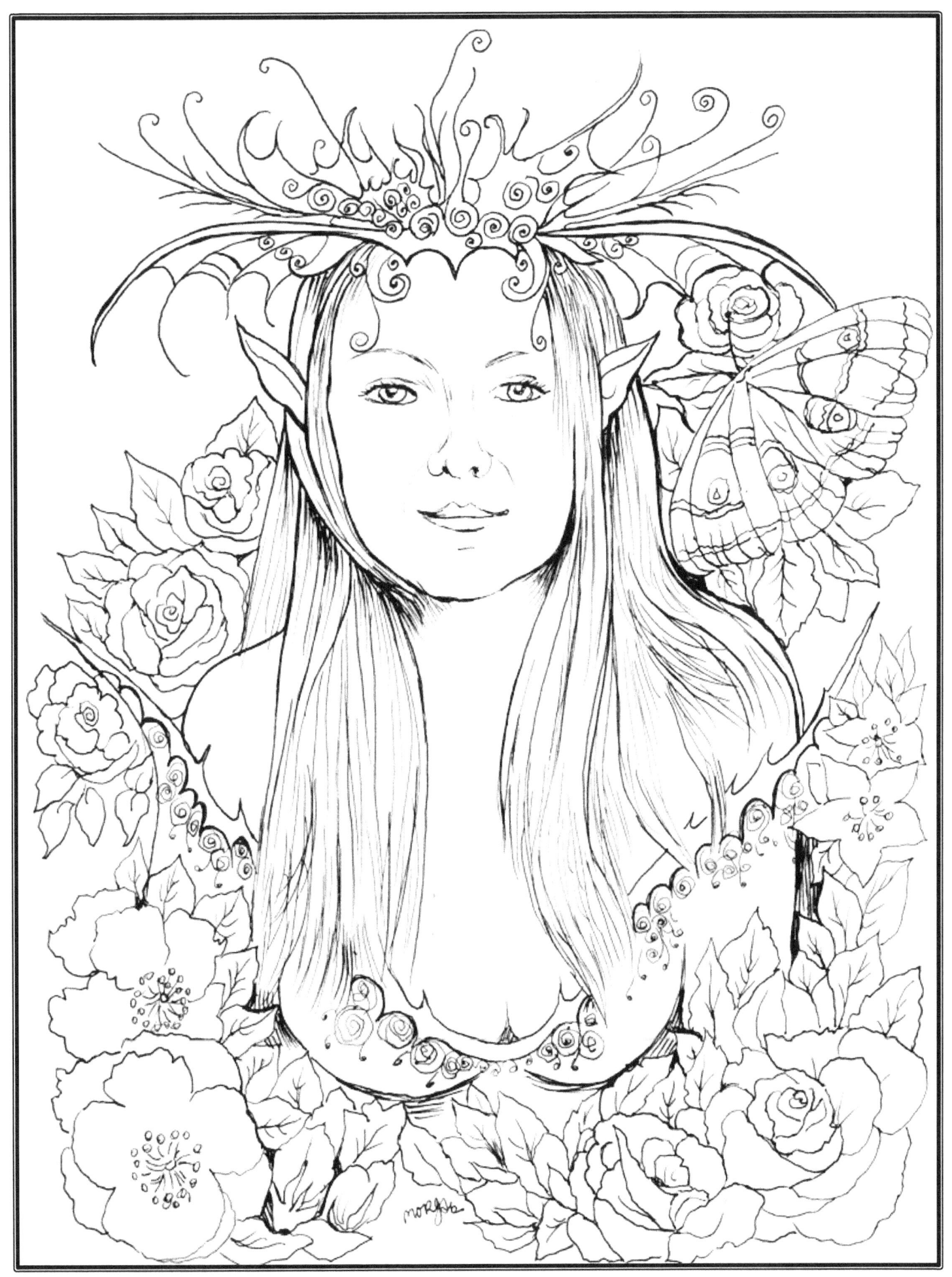

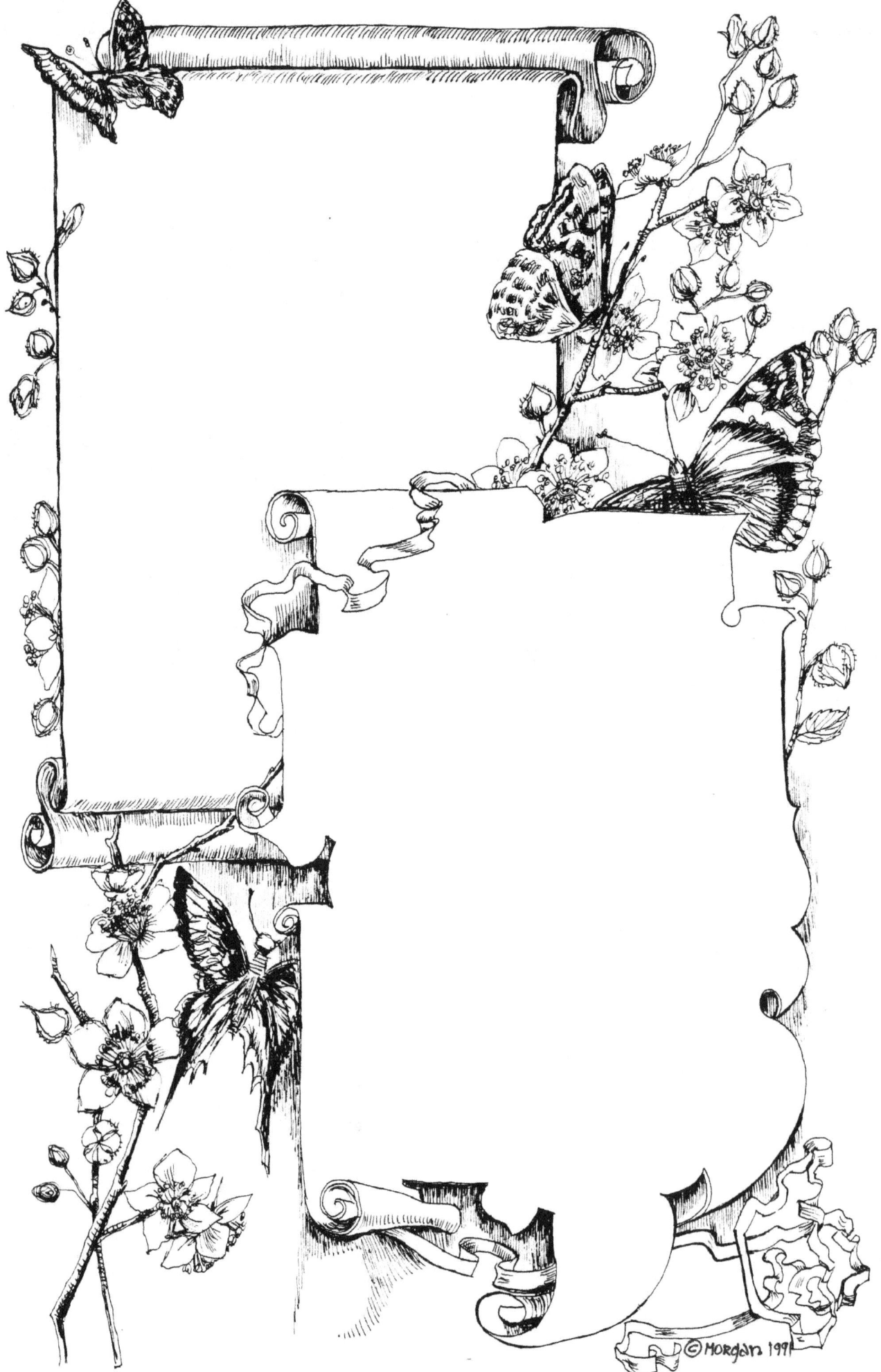

© Morgan 1991

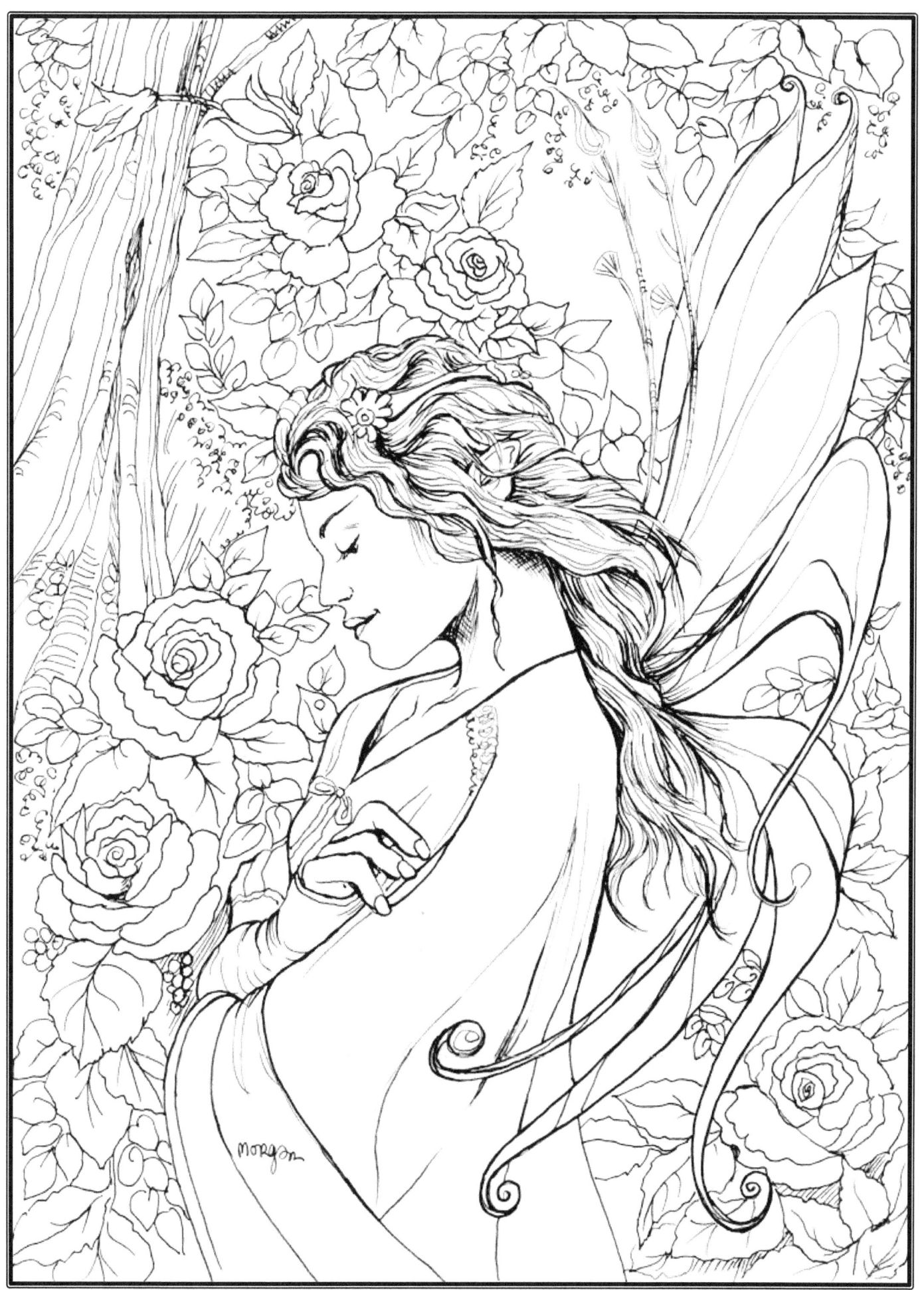

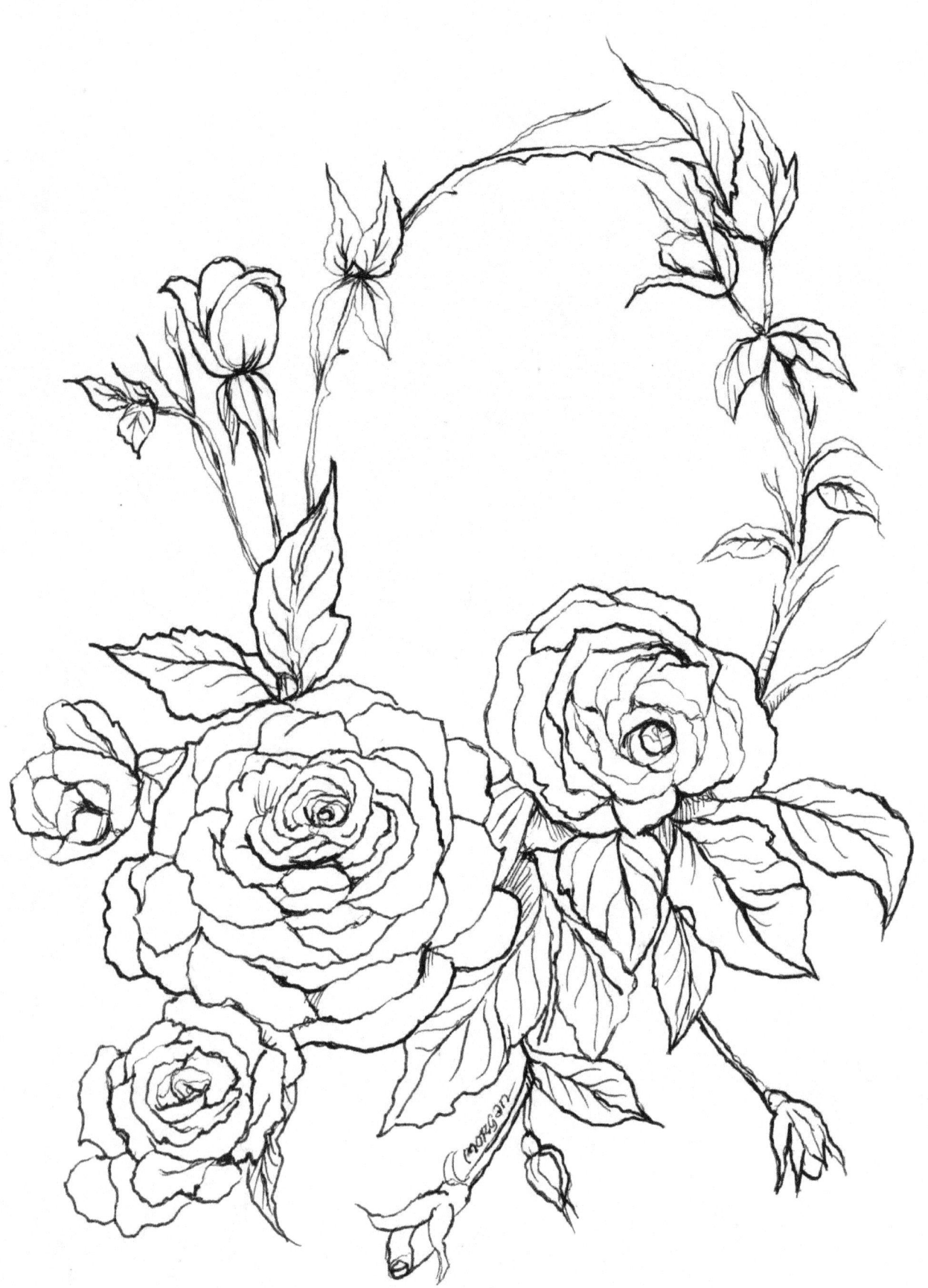

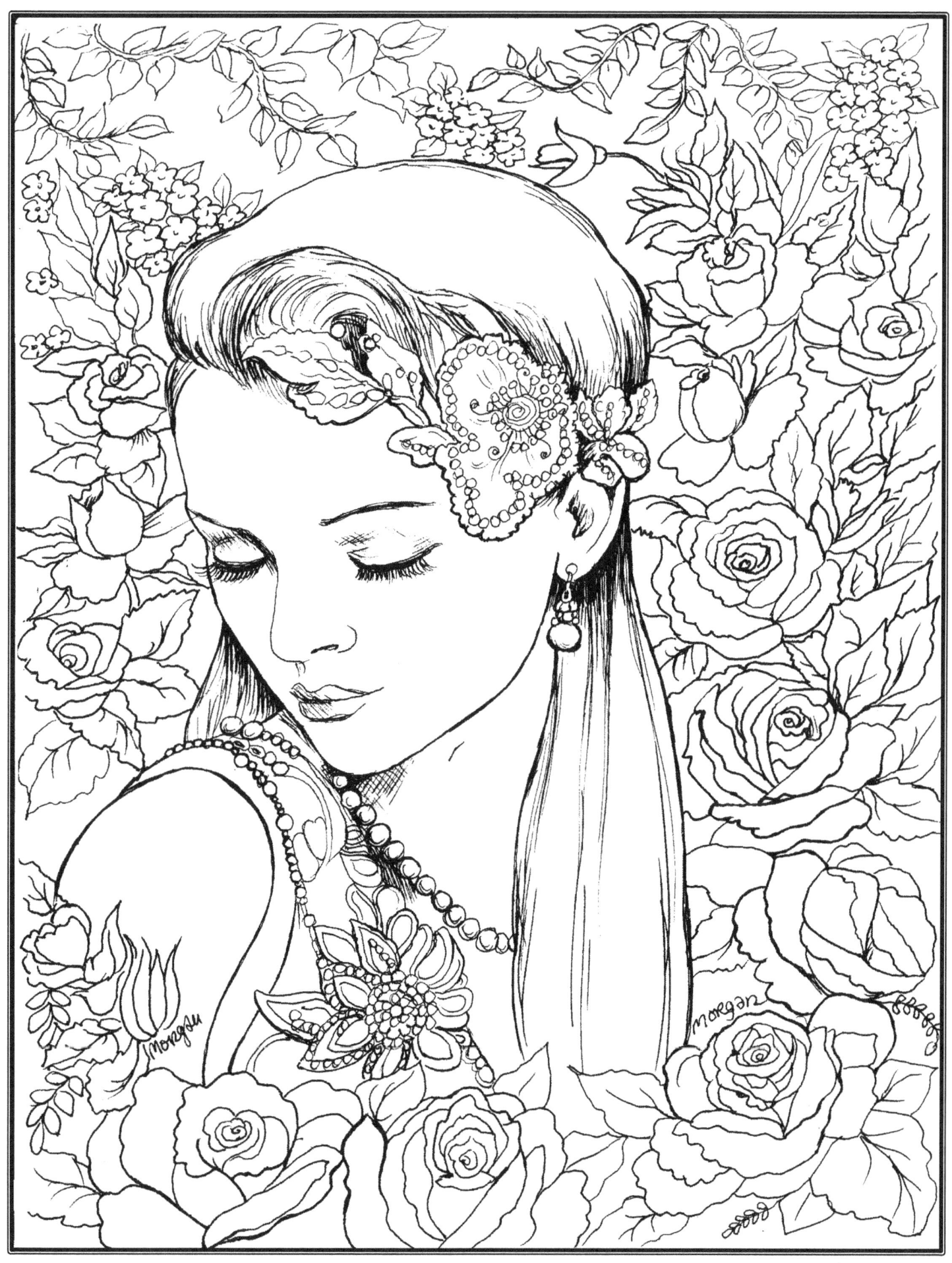

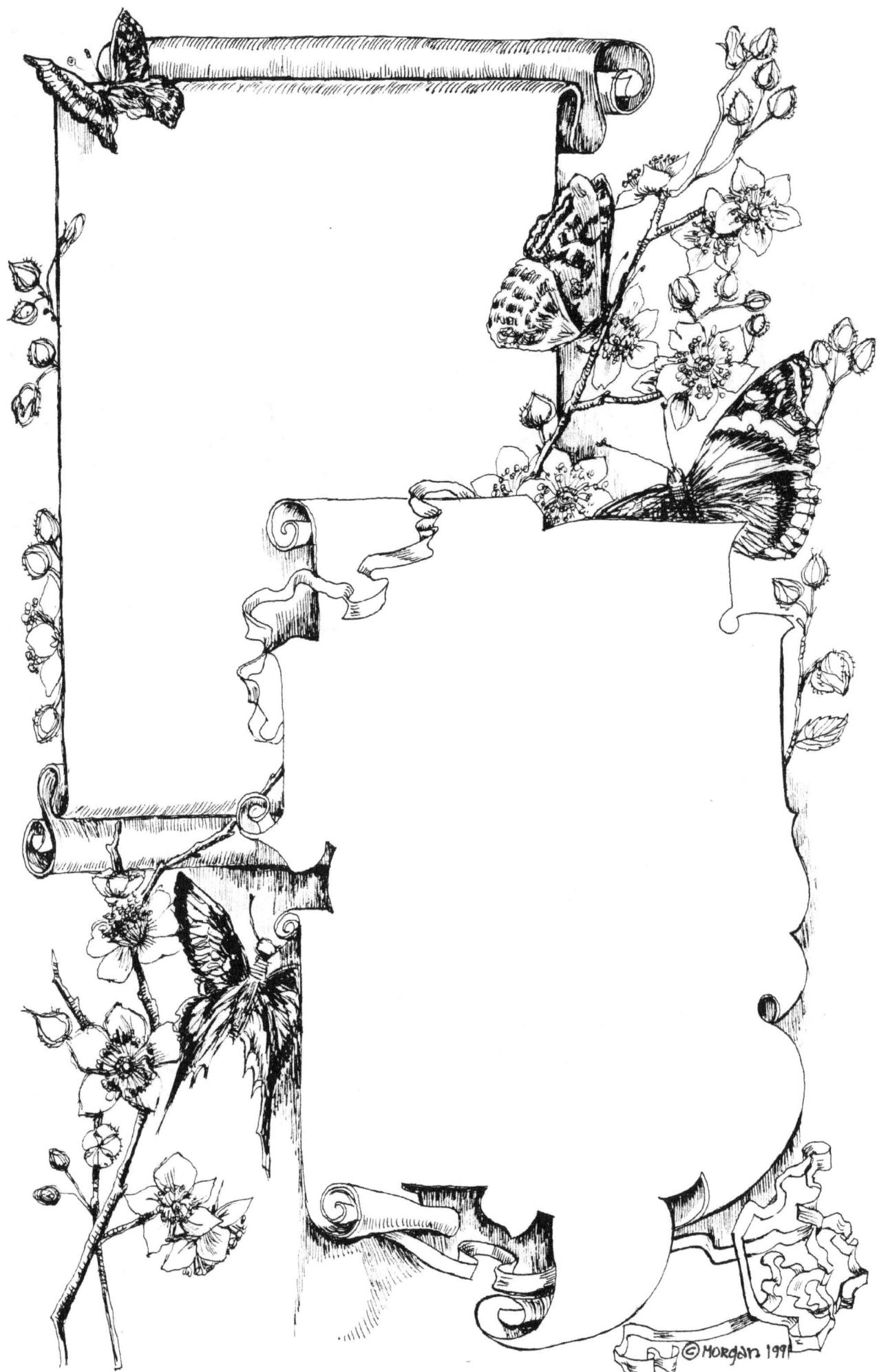

© Morgan 1991

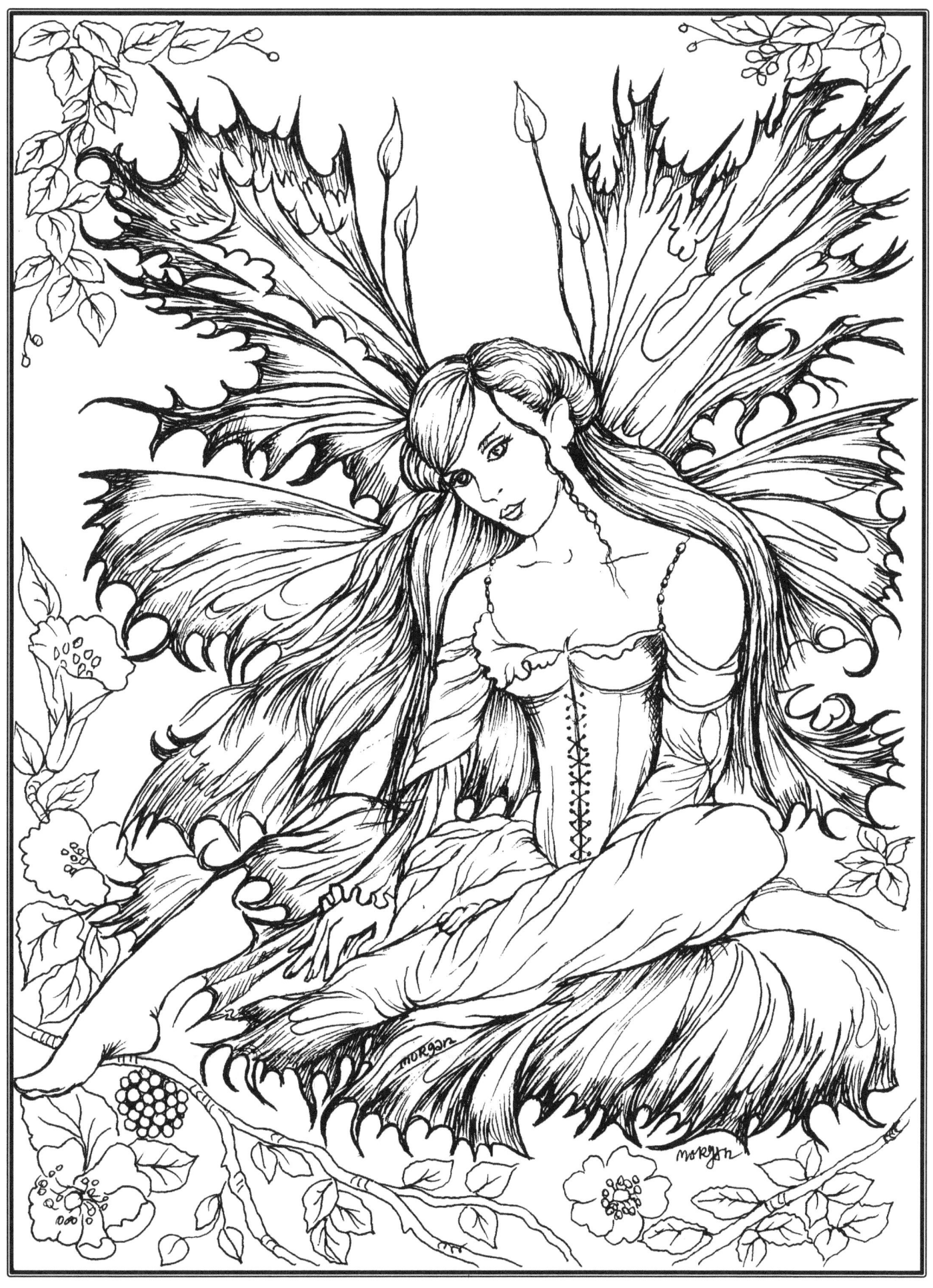

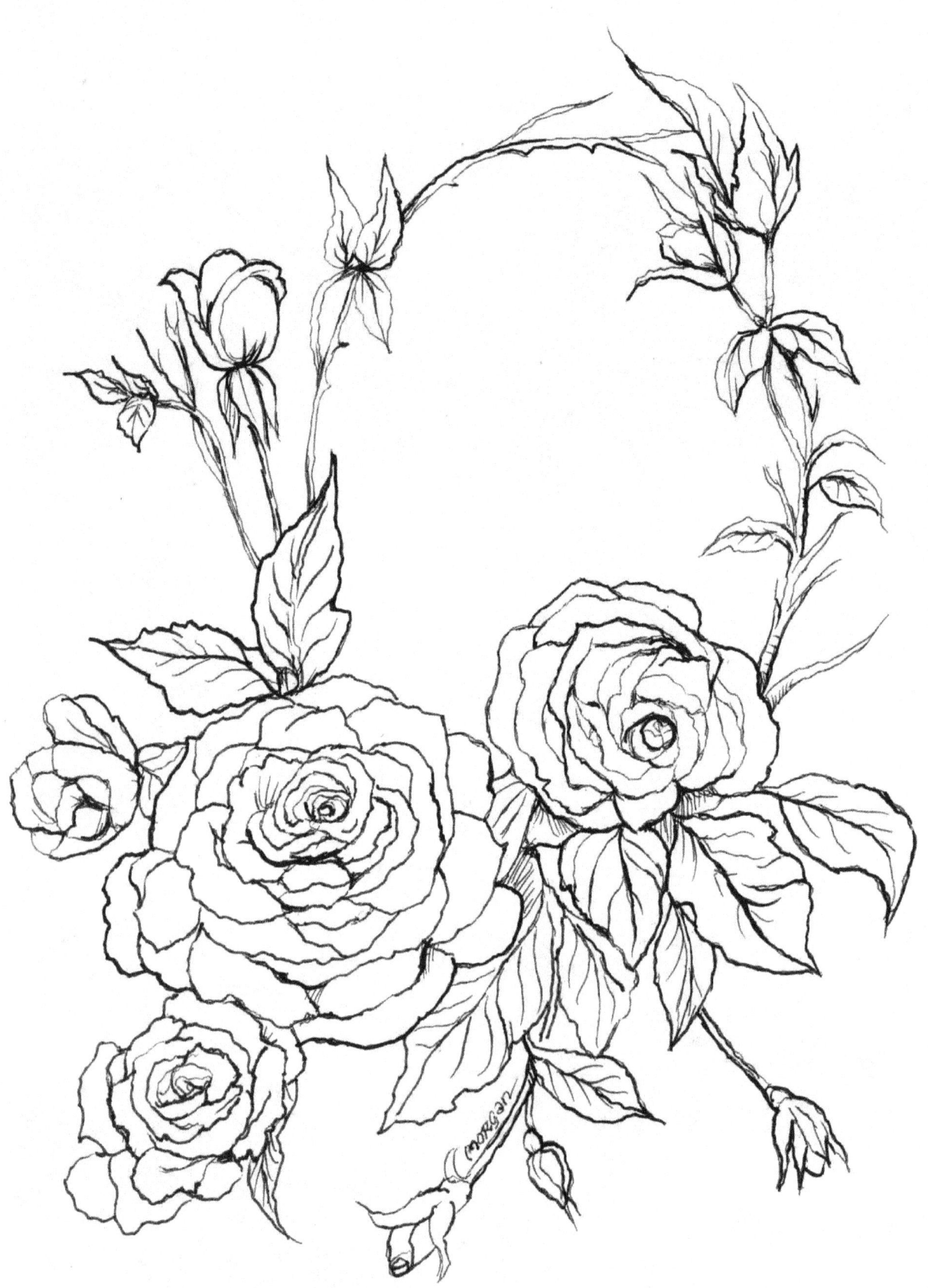

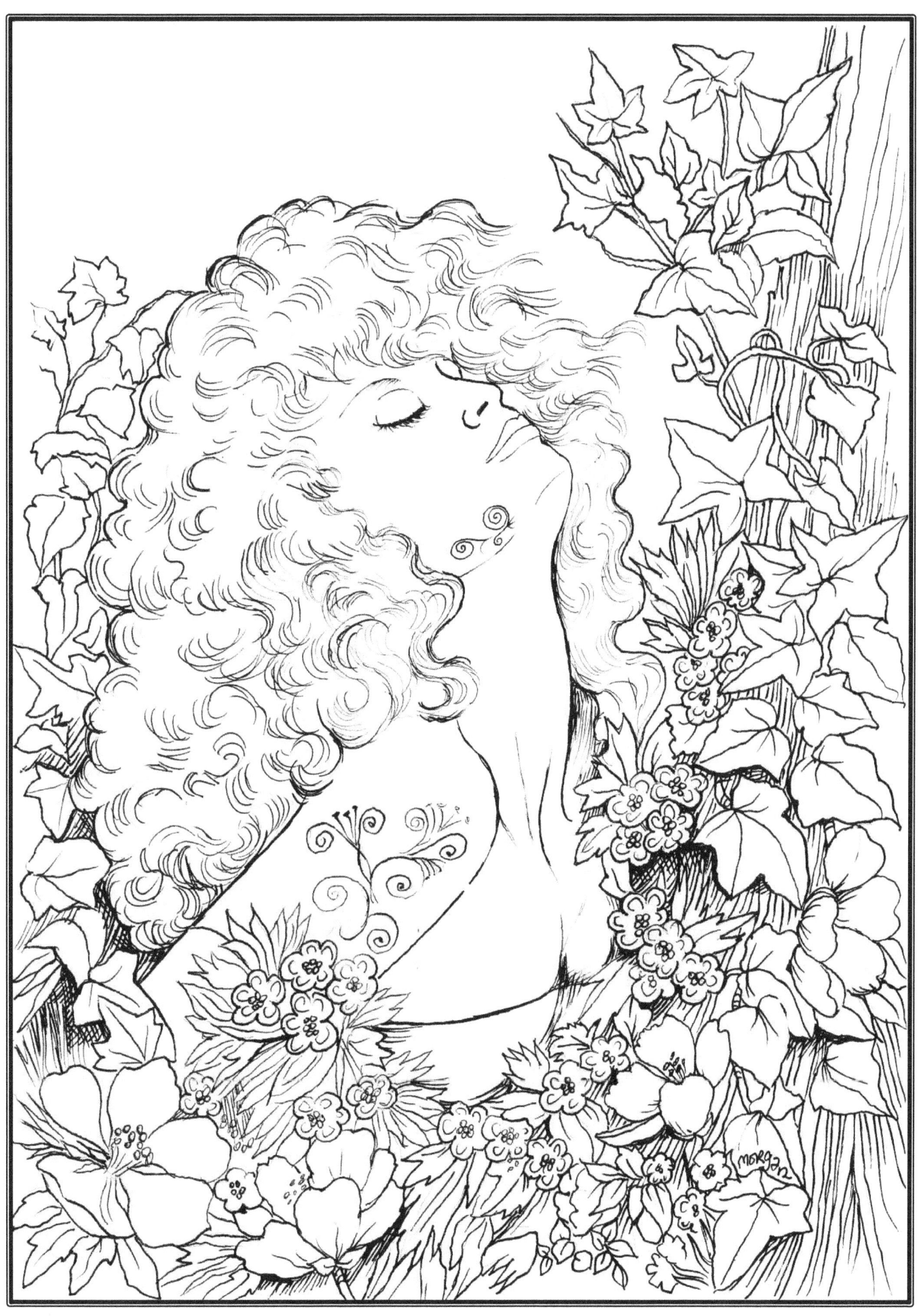

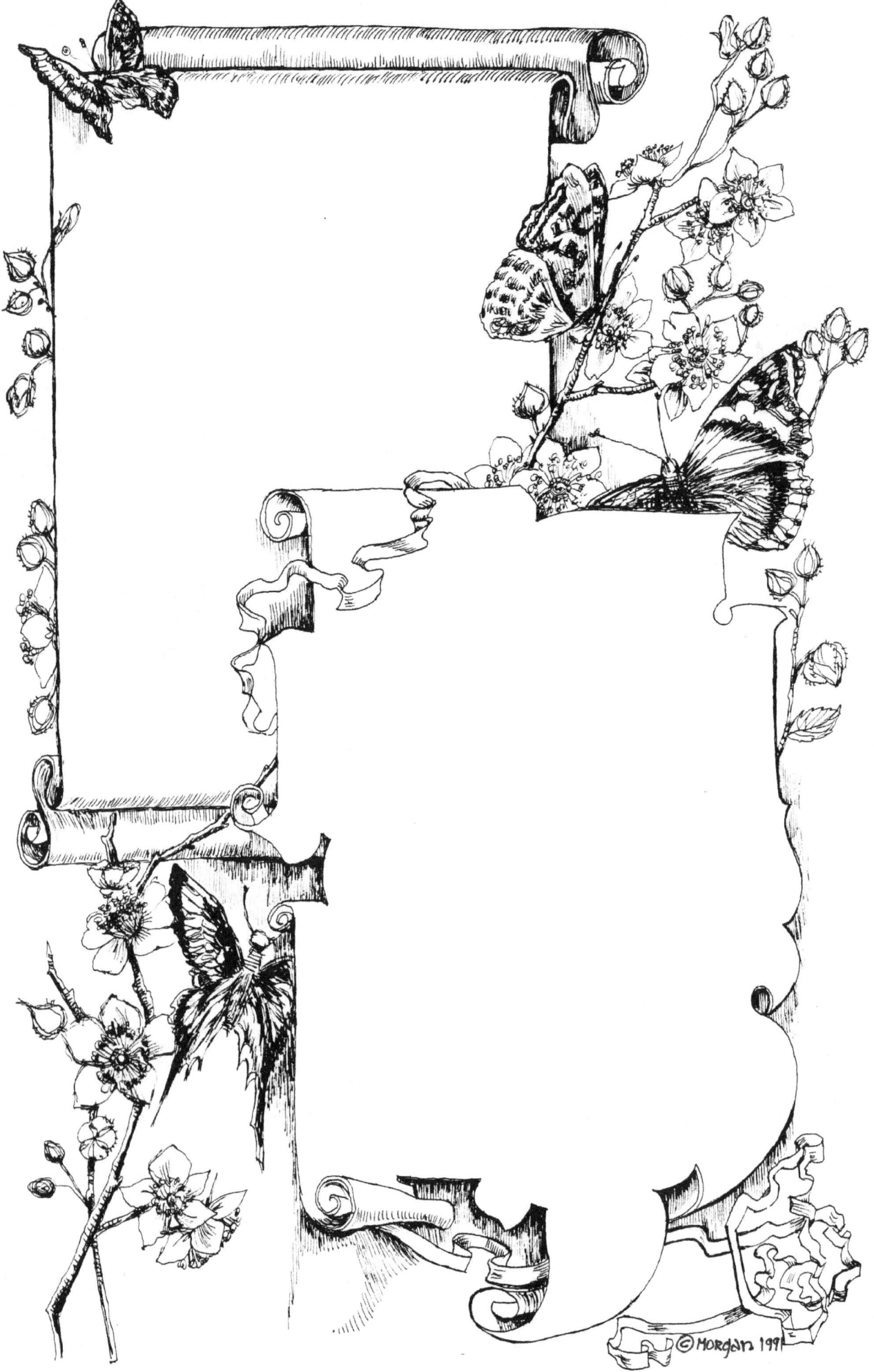

© Morgan 1991

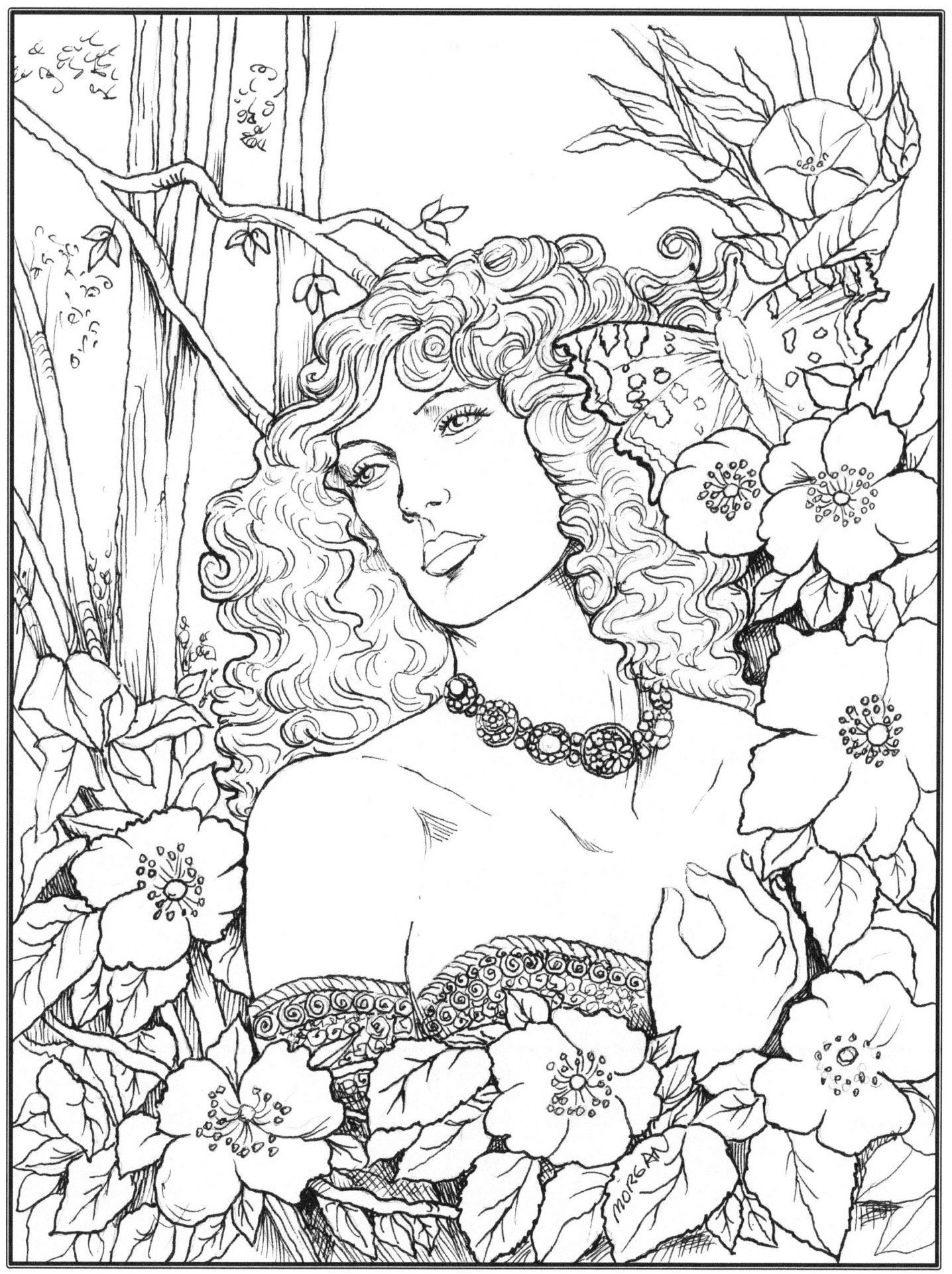

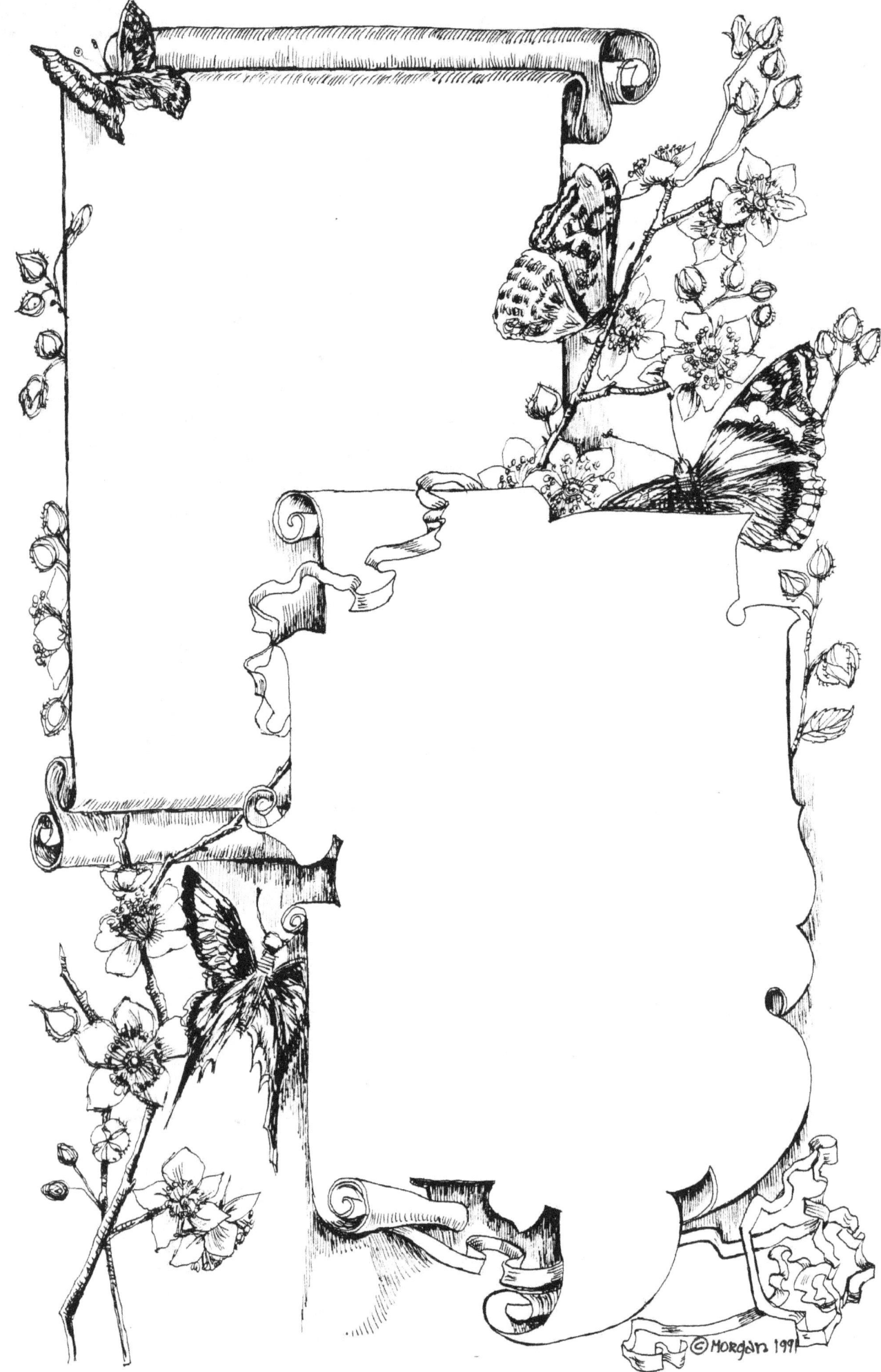

© Morgan 1991

www.ingramcontent.com/pod-product-compliance
Lightning Source LLC
Chambersburg PA
CBHW081020170526

45158CB00010B/3118